CRUMLIN GAOL

AN HISTORICAL INSIGHT

Window View. Crumlin Road Gaol. August, 2008. [Author]

Photo: Author

This Book is Dedicated to All Those:

"Who Walked Through the Tunnel,
No Matter Your District of Origin,
Your Religious Beliefs, Or Political Affiliation,
You Passed Through the "Crum".

A BELFAST CULTURAL & LOCAL HISTORY GROUP PUBLICATION

CONTENTS

Introduction 1

Chapter 1: A Brief Historical Overview. 5

Chapter 2: Political Conflict - 1865 - 1920. 19

Chapter 3: Partition To Armed Conflict. 1920 - 1969 45

Chapter 4: Armed Conflict To Peace - 1969 - 2007. 97

Chapter 5: Political Escapes From Belfast Gaol - 1927 - 1972 147

Chapter 6: Staff, Administration & The British Army. 173

Chapter 7: Closure And Regeneration. 191

This is a non-profit making community-based history project.

INTRODUCTION

When we embarked on this book, we knew from the outset it was going to be a challenge; not because of the subject matter, but purely on what we were going to include and what would have to be left out.

Being fortunate in the amount of material held in the archive of the Belfast Cultural & Local History Group, there was plenty to draw from, but the worst task is knowing you have to edit, or leave material out, while at the same time, getting a good balance in producing a book that the reader will not only find an easy read, but also an informative one.

Based on experience and success of previous publications, our aim has always been to produce Books and Booklets that are informative, and interesting, not a "text book" of facts and statistics that can lose the reader and the pleasure of a book that is an *"easy read"*, captivating their interest.

It has also been our aim to produce new material in our publications and approach the subject matter in a different style and this book is no exception to that rule.

The manner in which this new book has been approached, is to run parallel with the events of the conflict in Belfast throughout the twentieth century and how that in turn impacts on the history of the Gaol.

Crumlin Road Gaol, is an integral part of the history of Belfast, both politically and in a social context. When you walk the wings and landings of the Gaol, you are walking through the political history of Belfast; *it is interlinked*.

Chapter one is a summary of the Gaol's history, while the following chapters detail events in more detail.

The book intentionally outlines defining events in the history of the conflict during the years of 1920-1924 and again during the 1969-1971 periods of the recent conflict, or *"The Troubles"*, as it is commonly known.

They are important and defining periods in the history of Belfast.

It is a twin approach which enables the reader to gain an insight into the background of the conflict, while at the same time getting a similar insight into the history of the Gaol.

The book has also focused on the thirties and forties decades, which can often be overlooked in the bigger picture of the recent conflict.

There are some facets of history included, such as the valuable role played by a Belfast woman, a member of Cumann Na mBan in the 1918 protests carried out by republican prisoners, led by Austin Stack on B.Wing during December, 1918.

Within the same episode, there is the fascinating story of Patrick Leonard, a warder in the Gaol, who also played a leading role in aiding the protest, and who, a few years later found himself back in the *"Crum"*, under sentence of death.

While it is always mentioned that Eamon de Valera, spent a short period of imprisonment in the Gaol, or Rev. Ian Paisley, it is forgotten, or perhaps not known, that several men, who would become important figures, *"for good, or bad"* in the history of the Irish Free State, were imprisoned in *Crumlin Road*, in 1918, such as Ernest Blythe, Kevin O'Higgins, Gerald Boland, and Séumas Robinson.

Extracts from the private recollections of a former IRA Volunteer from the 1920-24 periods, provide a unique insight into Internment in the Gaol in May 1922, particularly the first day, and again the Internment period during the Second World War.

In addition, are the interviews and conversations with former internees from the forties and seventies period, which are held in the Group archive, which provide valuable substance to the story of the Gaol through their experience

The Gaol *from the other side,* acknowledges the price paid in lives by the Prison Service, and they are listed in the Book.

While covering the escapes from the Gaol, which are dominated by republican prisoners, we have acknowledged the two escapes by Loyalist prisoners in 1971, which have in the past been over looked by the sometimes*, audacious*, or "*spectacular*" republican escapes.

The nature of the northern state and its use of the Emergency Powers law, and Internment, have meant that the Gaol in the twenties, thirties and forties, from a political perspective, was very much a *"Republican History"*.

This only changes at the outbreak of the recent conflict, when Loyalists begin to enter the Gaol in any numbers from mid-1971 onwards.

This is by no means a definitive history of Crumlin Road Gaol, *if such a thing is possible*, it is as stated in the title; "***An Historical Insight***".

There are some elements of the history not included in detail, purely due to the format and regulated size of the book. This is not to diminish their importance, rather more a case of space and format.

We have also written about events that have not previously been highlighted, while at the same time making reference only to some, that have been well documented over the years.

We would hope that this Book will provide a valuable addition to the written material documenting the history of *Crumlin Road Gaol*, and will follow suit in the success of pervious publications.

Raymond Quinn
Belfast, Cultural & Local History Group
© January 2023.

CHAPTER 1:
A BRIEF HISTORICAL OVERVIEW.

On the 31st March 1996 the Governor of Belfast's *Crumlin Road* Gaol, Bill O'Loughlin, walked out of the fortified prison and the heavy gates of the *"Air-Lock"* slammed shut for the final time bringing closure to a 150-year history of imprisonment, conflict and executions. The Grade A listed building acknowledged as an outstanding example of Victorian penal architecture and planning was later transferred to the Office of the First Minister and Deputy First Minister in August 2003 for redevelopment under the Government's Reinvestment and Reform Initiative.

For most people in Belfast and across the island of Ireland, *Crumlin Road* Prison evokes memories of the recent twenty-seven-year conflict and indeed that link is very much justified through the estimated 25,000 people who found themselves within its walls for some period of time, whether as a result of Interment, or on remand of sentence as a political prisoner. The use of the prison to house internees was not a new concept as republicans were interned within the Gaol during the 1922-1924 period; again during the war years of the forties and then in the late fifties during the IRA's border campaign.

There is another history to Crumlin Road Gaol, one that in a sense has been overshadowed by the recent conflict and perhaps is forgotten; the conflict period of the twenties through the thirties and forties, which this book will reflect on in detail and hopefully open up a wider discussion around the 150-year history of the prison.

The **County Gaol** for Antrim [*to give it the original title*], was built in Belfast between the years 1843 and 1845 on a design by the renowned Sussex born architect and engineer, Charles Lanyon, to take over from the original county Gaol which was situated on

Antrim Street in Carrickfergus. Designated as the **District Bridewell and House of Correction for Belfast**, it was constructed on a 10-acre site at the bottom of the Crumlin Road [at that time a suburb of the town] from Black Basalt rock quarried in the surrounding hills of Belfast at a cost of £60,000, it was modelled on London's Pentonville prison and became one of the most advanced penal institutions in Ireland.

Built within a five-sided walled site, the Gaol had four wings radiating out in a fan shape from a central area known as the Circle [or Control Area]. This was copied from Pentonville's "*Radial Cellular System*" which at the time became a blueprint and was reproduced in 54 other prisons. The new Belfast Gaol also became the first prison in Ireland to be designed for "*The Separate System*" of confinement whereby prisoners were perpetually separated from each other and never allowed to converse.

The Gaol was built to house around 320 prisoners in single cell accommodation with each cell measuring 12 feet long by 7 feet wide by 10 feet in height. [However in later years and in more recent times, up to three prisoners could have occupied a cell depending upon the influx, such as during the early 1970's period.]

Of the four wings in the Gaol; A, B, C, D Wings, A.Wing was the longest with 31 cells on either side of each landing, of which there were three. There were originally 320 cells in situ, but after extensions to the Gaol were made in 1890 the total cells numbered 586. The extension work can be clearly seen today in the brickwork on the exterior of A Wing and on the inside of the front wall.

Other additions to be constructed between 1880 and 1890 were a prison hospital and the Laundry block, which were located close to A.Wing. Victorian Gaols were built as penal institutions and were "*working prisons*", so the laundry would not only serve the prison, but also the local community. Also in the building there was a tailor's shop and a boot and shoe shop where uniforms and footwear was made by the prisoners for the warders and inmates alike. Gas would have provided the main source of lighting and remained as such until electricity was installed in 1926.

The first official use of the Gaol began in March 1846, when under the control of its first Governor John Forbes, 106 prisoners; men, women and children, were marched in chains from the county Gaol in Carrickfergus to complete the handover of the two prisons. Of these original 106, six were already marked down for transportation to Australia or Tasmania.

Women were held in the Gaol until early 1918 and were housed in A.Wing then later in the prison Blockhouse located at the end of D. Wing next to the Mater hospital. Suffragettes were housed in A Wing during the 1913/1914 period.

The first political prisoners detained in the prison were from the Fenian Movement and the first political prisoner to die within its walls was William Harbinson. A former Colour Sergeant based at the Victoria barrack in North Queen Street, within a ten-minute walk from the Gaol, he was one one of many members of the Irish Republican Brotherhood [*founded in March 1867*] who were sent into, and used within the British Army for the purpose of recruiting for the movement.

With the knowledge of weapons and military protocol he possessed, Harbinson became a training instructor to the various Fenian circles, instructing them in the use of arms and military tactics. [*This same method of training was later used by the IRA*]

However, the hesitant policy of implementing those tactics and the refusal to give the word for action to thousands of men like William Harbinson and his comrades was one of the mysteries connected with the leadership of the movement at that time and left them open to harsh and prolonged criticism.

It is since been recorded that a member of the movement [An Irish American] is alleged to have passed on information to the British government of the activities and personnel of the movement and, in a subsequent lightening round-up around counties Antrim and Down, Harbinson and many of his comrades were arrested and interned in Belfast Prison. Another well-placed agent in Dublin was also believed to have been reporting to the British in Dublin Castle, the power base of British administration in Ireland.

This problem of agents and informers was many years later identified by Michael Collins as a crucial element that needed to be broken if resistance was to be successful and he set about in a ruthless but successful manner in breaking *"the eyes and ears of Dublin Castle"* during the 1920/1921 period.

While interned in the Gaol, William Harbinson died suddenly from an alleged heart attack on September 9th 1867. His remains were released from the prison and after a large turnout for the funeral, he was buried in the ancient monastic grounds at Portmore, Ballinderry, and County Antrim. Thus, William Harbinson became Antrim and Ulster's first martyr of the Fenian Movement.

Forty-five years later in 1912, a plot of ground was secured in Milltown Cemetery, Belfast and a monument in the form of a Celtic cross was erected not only to commemorate the sacrifice of William Harbinson, but also to act as a memorial to all those who served with him in the ranks of the Irish Republican Brotherhood and to those who had suffered with him in Belfast Prison.

Included among the seventy-two names inscribed on the monument are those of twenty Protestant Republicans who were members of the IRB and also the names of Colonel Kelleher, Captain John Dwan, Peter Healey and Captain T.H O' Brien, also Lieutenant's Patrick Hasson and Mark O' Neill, officers in the United States Army and all of whom were interned in Belfast Prison with Harbinson. These Irish-Americans had been members of *Clan na Gael* also founded in 1867 who had come to Ireland to take part in the Fenian Insurrection.

Some five years later following the erection of that memorial for William Harbinson and his IRB/Clan na Gael comrades, republican prisoners were again making their mark in the early annals of political history within Belfast Prison.

Republican prisoners held in the Gaol under the **Defence of the Realm Act** staged a riot in June 1917 over food and a force of seventy RIC personnel had to be brought in to quell disturbances, before the issue was resolved.

However, statements later given by men who were prisoners at the time, spoke of ill-treatment and brutality.

Political status had been won by republican prisoners, which at the time numbered between 200-250 men from through-out the island of Ireland.

But just as one crisis had been resolved, another quickly followed that same month of June 1918, when Influenza swept through the prison.

Austin Stack, the O.C of republican prisoners in the Gaol, recorded in his Gaol Journal that 111 men contracted Influenza, many of whom had to be moved to the prison hospital.

Then just three days before Christmas 1918, republican prisoners under the command of Kerry republican Austin Stack TD **- [having been elected for West Kerry whilst a prisoner in the Gaol]** were involved in a prison protest riot in order to ensure a republican prisoner, John Doran from Loughinisland County Down, was granted political status upon his sentence, in line with other republicans in the prison.

Doran's case became a concern to Austin Stack at the end of November following a previous incident when three prisoners had been taken from Belfast prison and treated as criminals upon sentence, despite the prison governor having recommended them for political status.

On Sunday morning, December 22nd 1918 following mass in the prison chapel, Doran, who was being held on D.Wing, was shuttled into B Wing by several republican prisoners and the wing then taken over by the prisoners.

Republican prisoners were housed mainly in A, B and C Wings, [C.3].

The protest lasted ten days until New Year's Day 1919, during which time the wing was wrecked for use in barricades [and until Doran's political status was assured]. This involved the heavy metal railings from B2 and B3 along with the wire netting, being smashed and thrown down unto B1, thus leaving the landings of B2 and B3 only as narrow ledges and dangerous for any attacking groups of RIC and military who had been brought into the prison.

Entrance to the Chapel on the Circle. Photo June 2009. [Author]

Negotiations which brought the matter to a conclusion had involved a priest, Fr. Mac Cauley, who also brought into the prison, the Lord

Mayor of Dublin, Lawrence O'Neill and the Rev. Dr. Mac Rory. Also involved was Colonel Eoin Lewis, Chief Inspector of Prisons.

Having achieved their objective, the prisoners were moved on to C.Wing and as a direct consequence of the protest, Austin Stack and several others were kept in solitary confinement until the morning of April 29th 1919, when he and nine comrades were removed from the prison under RIC and military escort and brought by steamer from Belfast to internment in England from where he later escaped.

The republican prisoners in Belfast may have had their spirits raised by the news of the escape of Sinn Fein TD Robert Barton from Mountjoy Gaol in Dublin some six weeks earlier on March 16th, 1919 and the escape two weeks later of senior IRB man Padraic Fleming also Piaras Beaslai, Thomas Malone and JJ Walsh TD along with sixteen other republican prisoners. Both escapes had been organised by Michael Collins. *They were not the first, nor would they be the last.* In fact, Michael Collins would also plan and organise Austin Stack's escape from Strangeways Prison several months later.

Collins had been keen to have Austin Stack *sprung* and had even planned an escape out of Belfast Gaol, but he was moved to England before the plans could be implemented. However, on the 25th October 1919 an IRA escape party which included Rory O' Connor, Matthew Lawless, Paddy O'Donoghue and Peader Clancy, implemented the successful escape of Austin Stack, John Doran, Piaras Beaslai - [*re-imprisoned following his earlier escape from Mountjoy*], D.P Walsh, Con Connolly and Paddy McCarthy. The men were brought to a safe house in the suburb of Prestwich, where they were visited by Collins who then made arrangements to have them smuggled back to Dublin via Liverpool during the first week of November.

[Austin Stack later opposed the treaty in 1922 and when Fianna Fail came into power, despite still being a TD, he refused to enter Leinster House. When he died through ill health in 1929 which was

brought upon by prison hardships, he still retained the post of Hon. Secretary of Sinn Fein.]

Republican prisoners continued to fight for the right of political status for sentenced prisoners during later decades of struggle and the first granting of political status in the recent conflict came about following an IRA hunger strike in the Gaol in May 1972 which was lead by the republican prisoners OC-[Officer Commanding], Billy Mc Kee and which also saw a severe and concerted campaign of street rioting and shootings throughout Belfast which reached their height on Tuesday 13ᵗʰ June 1972 as rumours –[*Deliberately circulated by the republican leadership as a tactic to mount pressure on the British*] spread, that Billy Mc Kee had died.

In April 1936 twelve leading republicans captured while in the process of conducting a court-martial at number 10 Crown Entry in the centre of Belfast, were tried under the old **Treason Felony Act of 1848**, which had been last used against the old Fenian Tom Clarke in the 1880's. The northern administration at Stormont had resurrected the Act rather than intern the men. *[Refer to the book - A Rebel Voice by Raymond J Quinn, 1999, for a detailed account of the affair]*

During World War 11, republicans were interned as a result of IRA activity and were held on D Wing. At its peak, their numbers totalled 200, with a large number of republican sentenced prisoners also being held on A.Wing.

D Wing, surrounded by barbed wire, was *"set aside"* from the other wings with one small door through to the prison circle. An elected "staff" of internees ran the wing and even controlled a separate cookhouse. Good order and discipline in the wing was the responsibility of the internees. Although they did not have to engage in prison work as convicted prisoners had to, they still had the hardships of prison life to endure, such as the poor food and unofficial assaults by prison officers who were supposed to maintain their distance from the wing.

The internees were however given much more latitude than convicted prisoners. They enjoyed social association from 7.30am until 8.30pm each evening before lock-up for the night. The exercise yard was open 3 times each day except in the winter, allowing sports such as Gaelic football, handball and general athletics. Their dining areas facilitated Irish language classes, a nightly rosary, meetings and parades. Military classes were also held, talks on strategy and gun lectures. [*This regime by the prisoners kept very much in line with that practised by internees during the 1920-1922 period at Ballykinlar camp and would be again used in Long Kesh camp in the early* 1970's] Mass and concerts would also be organised, all to help the mundane existence of men:

"who knew not of a release date and were isolated from families on the outside, many facing hardship with the added element of wartime conditions."

Above all, the men wore their own clothes and not prison uniforms, and maintained their own command structures to preserve discipline.

However, lengthy internment had a bad effect on the health of many men and upon release the fact they had been interned was noted on their papers at the Labour Exchange. There were also cases were the RUC exhorted pressure on released internees to move south or to emigrate.

When this policy of detention was implemented again in the late 1950's it was recorded that at the beginning of 1960, there were 166 republican internees housed in Belfast Gaol, along with 56 sentenced prisoners on A.Wing and 22 remand prisoners in C.Wing. The last of these men were all released by April 1961.

Internment was last introduced by the state in August 1971, when for the first time it was implemented by the British Army, but the northern state was reeling and the Nationalist people rise against it.

It turned out to be a disastrous and defining episode with far reaching political and security consequences. It sowed the seeds of conflict in the north and heavily influenced the turbulent events of the next quarter of a century.

Children were also imprisoned in the Gaol in the mid-nineteenth century for stealing items of food or clothing in a city where poverty in the working-class districts was rift. Sentences for children ranged from one week to one month and could include a whipping. That sentence could increase to up to 3 months if it was not a first offence, as in the case of young Patrick Magee, aged ten who found himself before the judge for a second time in April 1858 for stealing clothes from a *washer* woman.

Patrick was *"sent down"* for 3 months, a sentence the boy found to hard to endure resulting in him hanging himself within his cell on the 27th April 1858. Ironically, that same year a law was introduced forbidding children under the age of fourteen to be sent to an adult prison.

Over the lifetime of the Gaol, seventeen prisoners were executed by hanging and their bodies buried within the prison walls in unconsecrated ground the only marker being the men's initials scratched into the wall against the year of execution.

When Lanyon designed the Gaol, a gallows was not included and the first executions took place on an open gallows erected at the end of D. Wing in public view. The first *Condemned cell* was located in D. Wing and a tunnel was constructed running from the base of D.Wing across to the Mater hospital to allow a Doctor to walk over to examine the executed prisoner The spectacle of public executions ceased in 1860 and in 1901 a new execution chamber was constructed at the bottom of C.Wing and this was used until the last hanging within the prison in 1961.

Of the seventeen men executed between 1854 and 1961, fifteen were for criminal murder, one semi-political [Michael Pratley] and one [Tom Williams] for political action which resulted in the death of an RUC member.

The execution of nineteen-year-old Tom Williams on the 2nd September 1942 was the most emotive to be carried out in the history of the Gaol and was conducted by Thomas Pierrepoint. He would have been the most regular of the hangmen to appear in the Gaol carrying out six executions between 1928 and 1942, the last being Tom Williams.

No executioner was ever recruited from within the Island of Ireland, pre or post partition. The last man to be sentenced to death was another nineteen-year-old Belfast man, Liam Holden in April 1973. This run current with a young Loyalist prisoner, Albert Browne, who also had the death sentence passed on him, but on the 15th May 1973, the capital punishment law was brought into line with Britain and the death sentence was removed from the statutory books at the height of the conflict. With some 19,000 troops already deployed throughout the north, the Gaol full of political prisoners and any sense of normal law already a struggle for the British government to enforce, such an action would have created an even worst scenario regarding international opinion and added to the chaos of disorder.

When Charles Lanyon completed the Gaol design, he set to work on a design for the new courthouse built between 1845 and 1850. Situated opposite the Gaol, the building was topped by the figure of justice, the work of Dublin sculptor Boyton Kirk. [*The courthouse was enlarged in 1905, with new end blocks added, the recesses bricked up, and a stucco finish applied to the entire building. The amendments destroyed much of the detail of Lanyon's original*

***work*]** A tunnel linking the courthouse to the Gaol under the Crumlin Road was constructed in 1852 at 1.5 meters in depth. Its pathway was originally lined with cobble stones but these were later replaced.

No Gaol with a link to conflict is without its escapes and Belfast Gaol is no exception, despite the prison's heavy security overseen by the British Army stationed in the adjoining Girdwood camp. Several daring escapes were carried out by IRA prisoners during November and December 1971, but some 30 years earlier on the 15th January 1943, the IRA's Chief of Staff Hugh Mc Ateer and three other republican prisoners, leading Belfast republican Jimmy Steele, Patrick Donnelly and Edward Maguire, escaped from the Gaol, launching Belfast into the biggest security operation since 1922. A reward of £3,000 put on the men's heads was not taken up!

In total 37 Republicans and two Loyalists escaped from the Gaol between 1927 and 1981, thirteen of whom escaped within a six-month period during 1971.

In another piece of history, two republican prisoners held in the Gaol for their role in an attempted arms raid on the Depot of the Iniskilling Fusiliers in Omagh, were elected to Westminster in May 1955. Under the northern Unionist regime their mandate was not recognised as they were imprisoned, although they would not have taken their seats, as they would have been elected on an abstensionist policy of non-recognition of the British parliament.

Philip Clarke was elected for Fermanagh/South Tyrone and Tom Mitchell for Mid-Ulster. Tomas Mac Curtain and Manus Canning polled very high in Armagh and Derry, while Patrick Kearney stood in South Belfast at that time a strong Unionist seat.

Tom Mitchell having been disqualified despite winning the Mid-Ulster seat embarrassed the Unionist regime when he won the seat for a second time when a by-election was held on August 11th 1955. Mitchell increased his majority vote, but this was deemed ineligible and once again he was disqualified for being a prisoner in Belfast Gaol and the seat went to the Unionist Party.

Today, the people of Belfast and beyond are queuing up to *"get in"* through the gates of Crumlin Road Prison as its cells lie vacant, its wings silent and its yards only echoes are now from the builders, whose job it is now is to make this once penal institution a place of *"friendly"* restoration for those many visitors who wish to explore or *relive* it's historical; past.

Aerial View of Crumlin Road Gaol during the conflict period.

William Harbinson

CHAPTER 2:
POLITICAL CONFLICT - 1865 - 1920.

For a generation, Crumlin Road Gaol was very much associated with the recent conflict, when during the period from 1969 until the Gaol closed in 1996, around 25,000 people passed through its gates in relation to some kind of offence relating to the conflict.

But political prisoners have been a feature of the prison dating back to the mid-19th century and for periods dating to the early and mid-20th century. In fact, political prisoners and internees have been a regular cord running through the history of Belfast Gaol.

The first political prisoners detained in the prison were from the Fenian Movement and the first political prisoner to die within its walls was William Harbinson.

A former Colour Sergeant based at the Victoria barrack in North Queen Street, within a ten-minute walk from the Gaol, he was one of the many members of the Irish Republican Brotherhood [*founded in March 1858*] who were sent into, and used within the British Army for the purpose of recruiting for the movement.

With the knowledge of weapons and military protocol he possessed, Harbinson became a training instructor to the various Fenian circles, instructing them in the use of arms and military tactics. [*This same method of training was later used by the IRA*] However, the hesitant policy of implementing those tactics and the refusal to give the word for action to thousands of men like William Harbinson and his comrades was one of the mysteries connected with the leadership of the movement at that time and left them open to harsh and prolonged criticism.

It should also be recognised that Ireland was still reeling from the effects of *An Gorta Mor* - "*the great hunger of 1845-1849*" and its consequences which included the emigration of many of its people.

It slowly and painfully was in the progress of regaining some degree of normality.

It has since been recorded that a member of the movement [An Irish American] is alleged to have passed on information to the British government of the activities and personnel of the movement and, in a subsequent lightening round-up around counties Antrim and Down, Harbinson and many of his comrades were arrested and interned in Belfast Prison. Another well-placed agent in Dublin was also believed to have been reporting to the British in Dublin Castle, the power base of British administration in Ireland.

This problem of agents and informers was many years later identified by Michael Collins as a crucial element that needed to be addressed and broken if resistance was too succeed and he set about in a ruthless but successful manner during the 1920 / 1921 period in breaking *"the eyes and ears of Dublin Castle"*.

While interned in the Gaol, William Harbinson died suddenly from an alleged heart attack on September 9th 1867. His remains were released from the prison and after a large turnout for the funeral; he was buried in the ancient monastic grounds at Portmore, Ballinderry, County Antrim. Thus, William Harbinson became Antrim and Ulster's first martyr of the Fenian Movement.

Forty-five years later in 1912, a plot of ground was secured in Milltown Cemetery, Belfast and a monument in the form of a Celtic cross was erected not only to commemorate the sacrifice of William Harbinson, but also to act as a memorial to all those who served with him in the ranks of the Irish Republican Brotherhood and to those who had suffered with him in Belfast Prison.

Included among the seventy-two names inscribed on the monument are those of twenty Protestant republicans who were members of the IRB and also the names of Colonel Kelleher, Captain John Dwan, Peter Healey and Captain T.H O'Brien, also Lieutenant's Patrick Hasson and Mark O'Neill, officers in the United States Army and all of whom were interned in Belfast prison with William Harbinson. These Irish Americans had been members of the IRB's sister organisation *Clan na Gael* also founded in 1867 who had come to Ireland to take part in the Fenian Insurrection.

Burial Ground of William Harbinson Photo, 7th May 2009 [Author]

At the turn of the twentieth century a new confidence within Irish Nationalism, throughout the country reinvigorated the nationalist community of Belfast and beyond. The national revival of Irish culture, identity and the Home Rule campaign being intensified at Westminster saw nationalists begin to assert themselves. A strong base of political outreach linked with the social opportunity was taking shape in order to try and break the Unionist grip.

Within Unionism, this reinvigorated advancement of Catholic Nationalism in the north of the country, sparked sectarian propaganda, fear and suspicion, with animosity again coming to the fore with the Belfast Protestant Association directing this animosity

Austin Stack

into sectarian bitterness. Edwardian Belfast was a city of sectarian ethnocentrism, where the politics of *"Home Rule"* or the *"Union"* overshadowed the common need of the working class to survive.

It was the Home Rule issue that sparked most fear within Unionism and from this emerged a determined resistance mainly within their strong base of Ulster, which they considered solidly and homogeneously Unionist. This policy of resistance was to have a political stance supported by a newly formed group called the Ulster Volunteer Force [UVF] created to oppose Home Rule by force of arms.

This was countered by a similar Nationalist force, the Irish National Volunteers [INV] also "referred to" as the "Irish Volunteers" which was established throughout Ireland and in the main give its support to the Irish Parliamentary Party which in itself opposed militant republicanism in whatever guise. The Party also enjoyed the support of the Catholic Church and Ancient Order of Hibernians. The military element of Unionism and their overconfidence of holding Ulster had a catalytic effect on the growth of the Irish Volunteers in the north as it incensed nationalists of the western counties. Overall, in the north of the country, the new organization increased at a phenomenal rate and by May 1914 of the 129,000 Irish Volunteers throughout Ireland, 41,000 were enrolled in Ulster including some 18,000 in counties Tyrone, Derry and Donegal.

Both sides had created *"Citizen's Armies"*; however, the outbreak in Europe in August 1914 left the still unresolved "Irish Question" in a state of suspended animation. Britain worked the Irish Problem to its advantage, promising both sides a positive outcome at the war's end in return for their support in the war effort. Both groupings led by their political parties rallied to the cause, resulting in both forces being succumbed into the British Army. Not only had Britain defused a possible civil war in Ireland, but also it was now in control of both citizen armies turning them into trained and equipped Divisions within the British Army.

However, not all of the now renamed, National Volunteers were prepared to fight for Britain and a small percentage numbering several thousand, split from the National movement and re-organised themselves as the "Irish Volunteers" later to become *Oglaigh na hEireann* [Volunteers of Ireland]. The IPP still held the majority of support within the National Volunteer movement, which reflected that most nationalists even in the north hoped their policy and that of its leader John Redmond of supporting Britain's war effort might succeed in delivering a settlement which would prevent permanent partition.

But Redmond was to seriously miscalculate opinion in Ireland as he continued to call on Irishmen to enlist in the British Army, while at the same time Unionism had acquired new influence in the wartime coalition government at Westminster. The National Volunteer movement was falling into decline epically in the north, while the smaller radical "Irish Volunteers" began preparing for a rebellion against British rule in Ireland.

The events in Dublin at Easter 1916 with the rising would mark the beginning of the end for Redmond and the Irish Parliamentary Party. The revolutionary Republican movement struck a blow against British forces in Dublin in what became a *"blood sacrifice"*. It was originally conceived by the IRB as a national revolt, but with the struggle effectively narrowed to Dublin, military failure turned to martyrdom as the British engaged in harsh retribution. This retribution was to turn a population where a degree of hostility existed toward the insurgents, into a base of emotive support that was to see Sinn Fein become the motivating power in Ireland within two years.

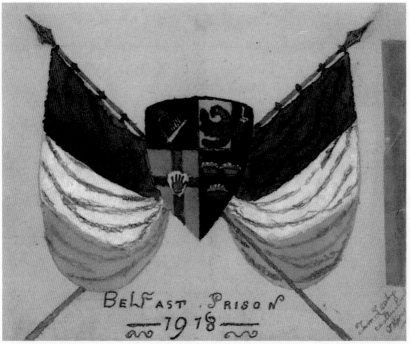

1918 autograph book cover of Republican prisoners from Crumlin Road Gaol.

It was against this background, that some five years on following the erection of the memorial in Milltown Cemetery for William Harbinson and his IRB/Clan na Gael comrades, republican prisoners were again making their mark in the early annals of political history within Belfast Prison.

Republican prisoners, held in the Gaol under the **Defence of the Realm Act** rioted on the night of 27th June 1918 over food and a force of seventy RIC personnel were brought into the prison by the Governor William Barrows to quell disturbances before the issue was resolved. However, statements later given by some of the prisoners spoke of brutality and degrading treatment.

Political status was won by the prisoners, but as one crisis was resolved, another quickly followed as Influenza swept through the prison.

Austin Stack, the O.C. of republican prisoners, recorded in his Gaol Journal that 111 men contracted the flu, with nineteen having to be moved to the prison hospital.

Then just three days before Christmas 1918, republican prisoners under the command of Kerry republican **Austin Stack TD - [having been elected for Sinn Fein in West Kerry whilst a prisoner in the Gaol]** were involved in a prison protest riot in order to ensure a republican prisoner, John Doran from Loughinisland County Down, was granted political status upon his sentence, in line with other republicans in the prison.

Dornan's case became a concern to Austin Stack at the end of November following a previous incident when three prisoners had been taken from Belfast Gaol and treated as criminals upon sentence, despite the prison governor having recommended them for political status.

The planned protest was relayed to Dublin and Kerry through messages being carried from the prison by members of Cumann Na mBan who would frequent the Gaol in a welfare capacity as many of the prisoners were from the south, making it difficult for relatives to visit.

Plans were also being discussed for a potential escape bid from the Gaol.

On a cold December evening, two weeks before the republican take-over of the wing, a young man clad in a black overcoat made his way along the busy compact through fare of Divis Street. Light snow trickled down illuminated in the gas lamps that cast light through the descending darkness that was quickly drawing in on the winter's evening.

From Mill Street, he passed *O'Hara's* public house and several small commercial shops, pausing at *Wordie's* Stables as a lumbering horse and cart rolled into the cobbled gateway.

With Christmas only two weeks away, there was an added feeling of a more than normal *ebb and flow* along the narrow busy street as women wrapped in shawls around their heads and shoulders, were busy among the little shops and in particular *Kelly's* poultry shop and the nearby Butcher's with their hooked chicken and

B3 Landing.

turkeys on display under their canvas coverings that sheltered the windows.

Crossing at Hastings Street, he passed the Irish National Forester's Hall, pausing briefly at Boundary Street as a Carter gave a burst of bodily effort and pushed his handcart over the cobbled street in his last shift of the day. He proceeded on; reaching *Magennis's* public house at the corner of Dover Street, were the sound of patrons could be clearly heard through the dim lite windows.

He glanced briefly at the Brickfields RIC Barrack on the opposite corner, before turning into the tightly bounded street of close- knit small terrace houses.

He did not have far to walk, just five doors before stopping at number 126.

His glove covered hand knocked at the door, as he shuffled the particles of snow from his boots, before being ushered into the small kitchen house.

The man was by now a familiar visitor to the house and was welcomed into the gas lite kitchen. Removing his overcoat to shake off some of the cold wet air, he stood in a uniform worn by the warders in Crumlin Road Gaol.

This was no social call, or a relative bearing Christmas gifts, but a caller bearing vital messages from Austin Stack of the impending protest set for Sunday morning, 22nd; only two weeks away.

The visitor on that cold winter evening was **Patrick Leonard**, a warder in the Gaol, one of five sympathetic to the republican cause.

The house he was now in, 126 Dover Street was that of **Nora Quinn**, a young woman, aged 20, who was active in Cumann Na mBhan and one of the main couriers between Austin Stack and Dublin GHQ.

It was from here that all messages were being communicated and all *outside* activity co-ordinated. Nora and a few other young women of Cumann Na mBhan, such as Nellie O'Boyle and sisters, Mary and Elizabeth McClean, were critical in that activity and pivotal was the man now standing in the house that evening, Patrick Leonard, a Galway man and four of his fellow warders.

Nora Quinn had joined the Republican movement in 1915 and was active in raising money for, and looking after the dependents of prisoners. She supplied personal items such as food, cigarettes, writing material and stamps at self -cost.

Nora made visits on a regular basis to the Gaol often with numerous letters, or despatches from Kerry.

She even opened her home to friends and relations of prisoners who travelled to Belfast from the south on visits which could be one of hardship in those early days.

Republican prisoners on the roof of B.Wing, December 1918.

Patrick Leonard had become the principle contact between Austin Stack and Nora.

Another *"friendly"* warder by the name of (*name withheld - Author*), carried two small revolvers and ammunition into the Gaol at great risk to himself, as part of a planned escape in a follow up to the Christmas protest.

Nora had bought the two revolvers from a British soldier.

The plans for this escape were smuggled out and brought by Nora to Dublin to an up-and-coming figure within the leadership with a growing reputation for boldness, Michael Collins.

The protest of December 1918 lasted for ten days, beginning on Sunday 22nd December and ending on New Year's Day, January 1st, 1919, during which time B Wing was wrecked for the use in barricades until Doran's political status was assured.

Heavy metal railings from Landings, B2 and B3 along with the wire netting were smashed and thrown down on to B1, thus leaving the landings of B2 and B3, only as narrow ledges and dangerous for any attacking groups of RIC and military personnel, who had been brought into the Gaol, [The military arrived on Saturday afternoon, 29th]

Some men climbed on to the roof of A Wing on the Friday afternoon of 27th December and planted the Irish flag, which attracted a hostile mob on the predominately Unionist Crumlin Road.

But after an hour and a half, they were ordered to come off the roof.

Republican prisoners were housed on A and B Wings, and also C.3 and numbered around 200 men. [A Wing would continue to house republican *sentenced* prisoners for the next 60 years up until the 1980's].

Around 75 men were involved in the *wrecking* of B Wing.

Negotiations which brought the matter to a conclusion had involved a priest, Father Mac Cauley, who was brought into the Gaol along with the Lord Mayor of Dublin, Lawrence O'Neill and the Rev. Dr. Mac Rory, Bishop of Down and Connor - [Later Arch-Bishop of Armagh]. Also involved in the negotiations was Colonel Eoin Lewis, the Chief Inspector of Prisons.

Having achieved their objectives, the prisoners were moved on to C Wing and as a direct consequence of the protest, Austin Stack and several others were kept in solitary confinement until the morning of 29th April, 1919, when he along with nine of his comrades were removed from the Gaol under RIC and military escort and brought by steamer from Belfast to internment in England.

But this is not the end of the story.

Michael Collins had been involved in the planning of two successful escapes of Republicans from Mountjoy Gaol in Dublin during March 1919 and was planning a similar attempt to be carried out in Belfast.

However, the men were moved to England before the plan, which would have undoubtedly involved Patrick Leonard, could be implemented.

This did not deter Collins and GHQ in Dublin.

On the 25th October, 1919, an IRA escape party which included: Rory O Connor, Matthew Lawless, Paddy O'Donoghue and Peader Clancy, implemented the successful escape from Strangeways Prison, north of Manchester city centre, of Austin Stack, John Doran, Piaras Beaslai - [re-imprisoned following his earlier escape from Mountjoy Gaol], D.P Walsh, Con Connolly and Paddy Mc Carthy.

When the men had breached the wall, Austin Stack was ushered into a waiting taxi and brought that evening to the home of a young Irishman called George Lodge.

The others quickly scrambled away on waiting cycles.

Aftermath of the Riot in B.Wing by Republican prisoners at the end of
December 1918. Picture taken on 2nd January, 1919.

The men were then brought together in a *safe house* in the suburb
of Prestwich at which they received a visit from Collins, who made
arrangements to have them smuggled back to Dublin via Liverpool
during the first week of November 1919.

Stack stayed at the home of Mrs Mc Carthy in Liverpool, before all the escapees were brought by Steamer back to Dublin.

Upon his arrival, he was brought to Batt O'Connor's home on Brendan Road, before moving again to 8, Lansdowne Terrace.

Austin Stack, from Tralee, had been Commandant of the Kerry Brigade of the Volunteers in 1916. He was arrested and sentenced to death for his involvement in the rising; however, this was later commuted to penal servitude for life.

He was released under a general amnesty in June 1917 and travelled home to Tralee with his friend Thomas Ashe. Two months later he was arrested again under **The Defence of the Realm Act** on the steps of the Liberal Club in Day Street, Tralee on a charge of drilling Volunteers.

Sentenced to two years imprisonment, he was moved to Mountjoy Gaol in Dublin were he led a hunger strike for political status.

Under a committee of five: Austin Stack, Patrick Brennan, Joseph Mc Donagh, Thomas Ashe and Michael Travers, forty men joined the hunger strike.

Despite attempts to break the protest through forced feeding and keeping the leaders in solidarity confinement in basement cells, they finally won through at the end of September 1917 achieving their goal.

But a high cost was paid for their success through the death of Stack's friend, Thomas Ashe.

Ashe was buried with full republican honours in Dublin's Glasnevin Cemetery with thousands of people lining the route from the City Hall to Glasnevin.

A firing party of eight uniformed volunteers fired a volley of shots at the graveside and an oration was given by Michael Collins as a huge crowd that had gathered in the cemetery, looked on.

Austin was appointed Secretary of Sinn Fein and elected as an abstentionist Sinn Fein M.P. for Kerry West to the Westminster Parliament in 1918.

He participated in the 1st Dail, the unrecognised parliament of the Irish people, and is widely credited with the creation and administration of the Dail Courts set up in parallel and opposition to the judicial system run by the British Government.

The success of this initiative gave Sinn Fein a large boost of legitimacy and supported their goals in creating *"a counter state"* within Ireland.

He later opposed the treaty terms of 1921 and during the civil war was captured by Free State forces, going on hunger strike for 41 days, before being released in July 1924.

When Fianna Fail emerged out of Sinn Fein as a political identity, he refused to enter Leinster House and stayed with Sinn Fein.

Austin Stack was re-elected on two further occasions to *Dail Eireann* as a Sinn Fein abstentionist candidate, remaining steadfast to the principles of republicanism.

He died in the Mater hospital, Dublin through ill-health on the 27th April 1929, aged 49, still holding the post of Hon. Secretary of Sinn Fein. He was survived by his wife of four years, Una.

Nora Quinn continued in her work with Cumann na mBan, active with prison issues and transporting weapons when required.

Weapons were often stored in her home during 1919 and 1920.

At one stage in 1919, she had:

Nine rifles, four Parabellums, [Lugers], two C 96 Mauser, semi-automatic pistols, nicknamed- *"Peter the Painters"* and Webley's in storage.

In this regard, she worked closely with Thomas Mc Nally, the Quartermaster of C. Company, 1st Battalion – [Later Colonel

Mc Nally]. C.Company at that time was based around the Divis Street/Pound Loney district.

He gave lectures on weapons in her Dover Street home to volunteers and these lectures involved Sean O'Neill, Sean Cusack and Rodger Mc Corley, who would play a prominent role in the Belfast IRA during the 1920-22 period.

As with Thomas Mc Nally, all three would hold senior ranks in the Free State Army after the end of hostilities.

Nora later married Kerry republican Danny Mc Carthy, who was involved in the 1918 protest riot. He originated from Castleisland, County Kerry and was the Vice-Commandant of the Kerry Volunteers.

The couple lived at Norfolk Drive, on the Glen Road.

Nora Mc Carthy-[nee Quinn], died on the 28th October 1970, just as a new and reinvigorated IRA was once more pursing the struggle against the northern regime.

Patrick Leonard, is a story in himself and certainly warrants further research beyond this book. Two years on following the end of the Christmas riots in Crumlin Road Gaol an attempted escape by republicans from Derry Gaol on the 2nd December, 1921 was foiled when a B Special stumbled upon the waiting cars at the prison wall in Bennett Street and raised the alarm with British soldiers who were on guard duty. They foiled the escape which resulted in the death of an RIC Constable and a B Special, William Lyttle.

As a result, two republicans, who were attempting to escape, Thomas Mc Shea and Patrick Johnson, of No 4 Brigade, Donegal, part of the 2nd Northern Division, were charged with their murders, along with a warder who aided their escape attempt, **Patrick Leonard.**

It is very unlikely, that there were two warders sympathetic to the republican cause from Galway, called Patrick Leonard, **this is the same man**, now up in Derry Gaol.

Thomas Mc Shea years later in his statement to the Bureau of Military History, Dublin stated:

> *"Leonard knew all about our plans and it was he who brought in the final word that the escape was to take place on the evening of the 2nd December."*

This again was very similar to his role he played between Austin Stack and Nora Quinn two years previous.

The three men were later transferred to Crumlin Road Gaol for trail at the Courthouse linked to the prison by the underground tunnel were so many men made the walk down through the decades, from cell to court, from court to cell !

In total, fourteen men were sent for trail as a result of the attempted escape.

Patrick was back in Crumlin Road Gaol as a prisoner and now in an even worst situation, as *"a condemned prisoner"*, for on the 12th January, 1922, all three were sentenced to death, their executions set to be carried out on the 9th February, 1922.

As no condemned cells were prepared in Crumlin Road, they were kept in the prison hospital for a few days, before transfer back to Derry Gaol by train under heavy armed guard.

It was here the executions were to be carried out by the British hangman John Ellis.

Thomas Mc Shea recalled how he saw a gallows being constructed for the execution.

But the death sentence imposed on the three men was to have serious repercussions at a time when the peace treaty between the Republican leadership and the British was still in its infancy.

On the 14th January, 1922, IRA volunteers were captured at Dromore in County Tyrone en route to Derry as part of a planned bid to rescue the three men.

As tension grew, the following month, on the night of 7th/8th February, a force of IRA Volunteers crossed into what was now termed as Northern Ireland from County Monaghan and took 42 Unionists, which included some B Specials, prisoner with the intent of using them as hostages should the executions take place.

However, at this stage through political negotiation which involved Michael Collins, the death sentence on the men was lifted, and commuted to: Patrick Leonard - **Life imprisonment**, with the two others being each given 15 years in prison.

But for the IRA, there was still the matter of the release of the men taken prisoner at Dromore.

Four days later, on Saturday 11th February, the situation took a critical turn when a train travelling from Belfast to Enniskillen stopped at Clones Railway Station in County Monaghan.

Clones Station after closure in the fifties.

In the past, this would have been considered a normal occurrence, but the geographics had now changed and this was a breach of jurisdictional boundaries, because on the train were eighteen armed B Specials bound for Enniskillen.

Their presence was immediately conveyed to the local IRA Headquarters in the old Workhouse and four officers rushed to the station by car.

The IRA commander Matt Fitzpatrick called on the Specials to surrender.

Whether in a state of panic, or feeling the need to defend themselves, the Specials, [or a Special], opened fire and Matt Fitzpatrick was killed.

Lieutenant Patrick Rooney who had served in the British Army during WW1, was walking behind Matt Fitzpatrick, when the fatal shots were fired from one of the train's compartments. He immediately emptied his revolver into the compartment before taking cover.

This then led to a barrage of fire from the IRA resulting in four Specials being killed and several wounded.

The IRA rushed more men into the area and the remainder of the Specials were taken prisoner.

The Northern administration in a fit of rage, called on the British Government to send troops into Monaghan and sectarian killing broke out in Belfast.

The IRA also brought more men into Monaghan fearing incursions from the Specials in a bid to carry out retaliation attacks.

Over the next few days frantic negotiation between the two sides quelled the situation and it was agreed that all prisoners on both sides would be released, which duly happened on Wednesday 16th [February].

Sadly, the bloodletting in Belfast continued with the Belfast IRA continuing a twin strategy of having to defend Nationalist Districts and when possible, carry out attacks on the Specials, which often led to reprisal attacks on innocent Catholics.

As for the three men whose sentence had been commuted, they once more found themselves back in Crumlin Road Gaol, [having been moved to Peterhead Prison in Scotland] were they remained with political status until their release a few years later.

In Later years, Nora Mc Carthy described Patrick Leonard, *"As a real good man"*.

He remained within the prison service in the new Free State, serving in different prisons until his retirement, settling in Lower Salthill, in his native Galway.

There were a few notable republicans imprisoned in Crumlin Road Gaol during the 1917 to 1918 periods which in conclusion warrant mention.

Terence Mc Swiney, who would become the Lord Mayor of Cork in March 1920, was returned unopposed for the first Dail in 1918 for Mid Cork.

He spent *a short time* in Crumlin Road Gaol, but had been previously interned in Reading and Wakefield Prison in England and then in Shrewsbury and Bromyard Internment camps.

He was arrested in Dublin on the 12th August 1920 for possession of seditious articles and documents, and four days later summarily tried by court martial and sentenced to two years imprisonment in Brixton Prison.

He immediately embarked on a hunger strike, which cost him his life after 74 days.

Terence Mc Swiney died on the 25th October 1920 and as with Thomas Ashe, his funeral attracted huge crowds in Cork City, were he is buried in the Republican plot in Saint Finbar's Cemetery.

Ernest Blythe, was born in Lisburn on the 13th April, 1889, and despite coming from a Unionist background, took a strong interest in the Gaelic language and culture.

He became involved with the IRB and the Volunteer Movement and as with did many others, found himself in Crumlin Road Gaol in 1918, were he took part in the B Wing protest riots.

He was returned to the first Dail as a Sinn Fein TD – [*Teachta Dala*] for Monaghan North during the 1918 Westminster elections, to which, as with all elected Sinn Fein candidates, he abstained.

A strong supporter of the treaty, he became Minister for Finance in 1922 in the *Cumann na n Gaedheal* government led by William Cosgrave.

He was one of the architects of the Free State Cabinet who endorsed partition through recognition of the northern state and opposed any IRA action in the north, saying Nationalists there should accept the regime.

He lost his seat in 1933 when Fianna Fail came to power and he joined the National Guard - [*"Blueshirts"*] led by Eoin O 'Duffy.

That same year, *Cumann na n Gaedhael* joined with the *National Centre Party* and became Finn Gael in opposition to Fianna Fail, shaping politics in the south for many years to come.

Blythe retired from politics and became the Managing Director of the Abbey Theatre in Dublin between 1941-1967, were he maintained his love of the Irish language.

He died aged 85 at his home in Phibsborough, Dublin on the 23rd February, 1975, living to see republicans rising again in the north and the downfall of the Northern Ireland Parliament in 1972; the same parliament he had tried to convince northern Nationalists to give allegiance to in 1922.

He is buried in Glasnevin Cemetery, Dublin.

Another person of note, who spent a period of time in the Gaol during 1918, was **Kevin O'Higgins**.

Born in Stradbally. County Laois on the 7th June, 1892, Kevin O'Higgins joined the Stradbally Company of the volunteers in 1915.

He found himself in Crumlin Road Gaol arrested under the Defence of the Realm Act in 1918. He was elected as a TD to the first Dail, but is not listed among the men who participated in the B Wing riots in Austin Stacks Gaol Journal.

As with Ernest Blythe, he supported the treaty and was a member of the first *Cumann na n Gaedheal* Cabinet in 1922.

He proved a very controversial figure and is remembered as the minister who signed the execution orders of seventy-seven republicans during the civil war period, which included that of Rory O'Conner, who was the *Best Man* at his wedding.

Considered to be a very capable politician, his legacy is marred by his ruthless treatment of republicans and betrayal of the IRA Northern Divisions.

He would also have been a critic of the support being given by Michael Collins to republicans in the north by continuing to supply them weapons up until the beginning of the civil war.

However, this mindset was to seal his own execution by the IRA, who would not forget his brutality.

His hour of reckoning came on Sunday morning, 10th October, 1927, when having walked from his home at Cross Avenue, Blackrock to attend mass, he had gone the short distance to the junction of Booterstown Avenue, when three IRA volunteers stepped forward, opening fire.

The fatal shots were fired by Archie Doyle, Tim Coughlan and Bill Gannon. Republican justice was seen to be done for the seventy-seven executed prisoners.

Archie Doyle lived until 1980 and until his final days, he never regretted his role in the death of O'Higgins.

Séumas Robinson was born in Sevastopol Street, Belfast on the 6th January, 1890 into a republican family background.

Along with his older brother Joseph, he joined the first Belfast Fianna Eireann *Sluagh* created by Bulmer Hobson in 1902.

A year later, the family moved to the Govan hill district of Glasgow, an area of the city that has always been associated with migration.

The Robinson brothers became involved with the Gaelic League and then the volunteers in 1913, although Seamus spent a period of his early adulthood in a seminary as a monk.

Seamus along with other volunteers made their way to Ireland to take part in the rising of 1916, resulting in his Internment in Frongach Camp.

While interned he became friendly with a Tipperary volunteer, Eamon O'Dwyer and upon their release he travelled to Tipperary, becoming active again in the volunteers while working as a Farm-Hand at O'Dwyer's in *Kilshenane*, which was an active location used by the volunteers.

He was imprisoned again in 1918 under the Defence of the Realm Act and found himself back in the city of his birth, Belfast.

Seamus was involved in the June 1918 protests in Crumlin Road Gaol, but was released before the December riots of that year in B Wing.

Returning to Tipperary, he participated in the *Soloheadbeg* ambush on the 21st January, 1919, designed to provoke the public mood into an impending war.

[Refer to Chapter 3].

Séumas Robinson, now a *"Wanted Man"*, participated in a number of attacks on Crown forces in Dublin, before returning to Tipperary in December 1919, to command the 3rd Tipperary Brigade in a series of attacks against RIC Barracks in 1920.

He was elected to Dail Eireann in 1921 as a Sinn Fein TD for Waterford-Tipperary East and opposed the treaty during the civil war period.

Following the end of the civil war, he resigned from Sinn Fein and helped in the foundation of the new Fianna Fail party and served three terms in Seanad Eireann; 1928, 1931 and 1934, before his death in Dublin on 8th December, 1961, aged 72.

Another prominent figure who was imprisoned in Crumlin Road Gaol as a young man in 1917, was **Gerard Boland** one of the founding members of Fianna Fail.

Born on the 25th May, 1885, into a staunch Nationalist family, Gerard along with his two brothers, Harry and Ned, became involved with the IRB and the Irish Volunteer Movement. [His sister Kathleen was also an active member of Cumann Na mBan]

He, along with both his brothers, participated in the Easter Rising, serving at Jacob's Mill under Thomas Mac Donagh. Following the surrender of the insurgents, Gerard Boland was interned in Frongoch Internment camp in Wales.

Following his release in December, 1916 under the general amnesty, he remained with the volunteers, but declined to re-join the IRB.

He was re-arrested in 1917, under The Defence of the Realm Act for practising military drills in the Dublin Mountains and imprisoned in Crumlin Road Gaol between June and December 1917.

During the War of Independence, he served in the 3rd Battalion, [South Dublin] Brigade, IRA and would have been considered "*Socialist*" in his thinking and political outlook.

All three Boland brothers opposed the treaty, and Gerard spent time in prison during the civil war. His brother, Harry was a close friend of Michael Collins and a TD in both the 1ˢᵗ and 2ⁿᵈ Dail. Harry was shot unarmed in the Grand Hotel in Skerries by two Free State Army officers, who went there to arrest him on 1ˢᵗ August, 1922.

He died the following evening at 9pm in St.Vincent's Hospital, Dublin.

Kevin O' Higgins refused Gerard parole to attend the funeral.

Gerard Boland helped to re-build Sinn Fein after the civil war, but along with Eamon de Valera left the party in 1926 over the policy not to take their seats in the Dail.

He was prominent along with Sean Lemass in building grassroots support for the new *Fianna Fail* party led by Eamon de Valera and when they defeated *Cumann na nGaedheal* in the 1932 election, he took up his first ministerial post.

He would become the longest serving Minister for Justice in the Dail, a post he first held from 1939 to 1948. It was this appointment that was to prove the most controversial and certainly one that republicans will not forget regarding the career of Gerard Boland.

Gerard Boland took a very hard-line approach on IRA activity during the war years of 1939-1945. He ordered several hundred republicans to be interned; set up military and special criminal courts and had six republicans executed.

He also allowed two IRA volunteers to die on hunger strike in 1940.

Ironically, this was done by a party who referred to themselves in their very name, as a *"Republican Party"*.

Gerard Boland's son Kevin, followed his father into politics and will be remembered by those familiar with Irish politics and history, for his resignation from government in 1970 over the *"Arms Trial"* debacle, in which ministers Charles Haughey and Neil Blaney were accused of being involved in attempting to import and send weapons to the north to defend Nationalist districts.

Both men were sacked from the cabinet, but later acquitted of the charges.

Kevin Boland resigned from the government in sympathy with the two ministers, and both he and Neil Blaney resigned their membership of Fianna Fail and continued to support the Nationalist cause in the north.

Gerard Boland died in 1973 and is buried in the Republican plot in Glasnevin Cemetery in Dublin.

His brother Harry is also buried in the plot next to Cathal Brugha.

Of the two brothers, Harry would be remembered in a more favourable light.

He served with the 2nd Battalion of the Dublin Brigade during the rising and as a result spent time in both Dartmore and Lewes prison, before his release in 1917.

His tailoring shop at 64 Middle Abbey Street had a concealed armoury were rifles were stored and it was often used by the Dublin Brigade, including the ASU.

Harry was close to both De Valera and Michael Collins.

He was a good political organiser, charismatic and also genial and good-humoured in nature. During the civil war, he took part in the fighting in Dublin and Blessington-[As did Gerard].

Harry Boland was also featured as one of the major characters in the Michael Collins movie, starring Liam Neeson; Harry Boland's part being played by Aidan Quinn.

CHAPTER 3:
PARTITION TO ARMED CONFLICT. 1920 - 1969

On a cold January Tuesday morning in 1919, a group of eight men sat in deep conversation in an abandoned house, known locally as the *"Tin Hut"* in the town land of Greenane, Templenoe, in rural Tipperary.

But this was no social gathering, as the group under the command of Belfast born, Séumas Robinson, discussed the various scenarios that lay before them in the coming hours.

These men; Séumas Robinson, Sean Treacy, Dan Breen, Sean Hogan, Patrick O'Dwyer and Tadgh Crowe, were volunteers drawn from C and E Companies of the local Volunteer Battalion and the discussions centred on an impending ambush of an RIC protected crate of gelignite that was being consigned from the British Army barracks at Templemore to the quarry at Soloheadbeg.

They were debating the strength of the RIC escort; would it be two men, or six, perhaps more, this was the main topic of conversation that dictated their plan of action as they proceeded toward the quiet Tipperary roadway that led to the quarry.

As it materialised, the horse drawn cargo consisted of two RIC men; Constable's, Mc Donnell and O'Connell armed with carbine rifles.

Taken by surprise, in the ensuing confrontation, both men were shot by the volunteers and the gelignite captured for distribution to the local Companies.

The fact that the Soloheadbeg ambush has taken on disproportionate importance due to its coincidence with the meeting of the first Dail in the Mansion House in Dublin, it is commonly presented as the *"opening shots,"* of what is termed as the War of Independence in Ireland, or *Cogadh na Saoirse*, between 1919-1921.

Séumas Robinson 1922

The action at Soloheadbeg was the product of a local initiative rather than a timely political action from any central command.

In fact in those very early days the volunteers often acted under their own control, rather than taking direction from the Dail.

But for some people in Dublin GHQ such as Michael Collins, the action of the volunteers in Tipperary sounded a note of military intent that they were keen to push further into a widespread campaign of attacks against the RIC, who were the *"eyes and ears"* of the Crown, especially in the country regions.

The men were brought to Dublin by Collins, to avoid the manhunt now in place in Tipperary.

Upon arrival in the city, Séumas Robinson and Sean Treacy were brought by Kathleen Boland to the Boland home at Clontarf for a few days, while she organized safe houses for them. She picked them up from her brother's [Harry], tailoring shop in Middle Abbey Street, which was frequently used by the Dublin Brigade and would later have a secret build in armoury stocked with rifles.

The war would take another year and half before it reached the streets of Belfast, but when it did, it would be one of concerted sectarian brutality and violence that would cost the lives of upwards of 500 people, with several hundred more injured.

In July 1920, sectarian warfare broke out on the streets of east and west Belfast, mainly concentrated in the Ballymacarrett and Clonard districts.

Concerted violent attacks were made on both areas by strong Unionist mobs intent in destroying homes, Catholic owned public houses and business premises.

Nineteen people were killed over the following week as the war reached Belfast with its in-trenched sectarian history and Unionist pogroms.

On the afternoon of 22nd July, 1920 at 4pm, hundreds of Unionists from the Newtownards Road launched an attack against the Nationalist side of Ballymacarrett, surging down Bryson Street to attack the Catholic area of Comber Street, Kilmood Street and Seaforde Street.

Desperate hand to hand fighting ensued as the residents rallied and forced the mobs back up Bryson Street. The British Army opened fire with a Lewis machine –gun, sending several bursts over the heads of both the attacking mob and the defending residents.

After a short interval, a much larger crowd of several thousand again launched toward St. Matthew's church on the Newtownards Road and the near-by Cross and Passion Convent, intent in burning both buildings.

Once more, local residents rallied, pushing back the mobs, before soldiers of the Norfolk Regiment opened fire in the church grounds, killing three of the crowd, two of whom were women; one aged fifteen.

The same regiment also opened fire in the Clonard district firing down Cupar Street and Kashmir Road as Clonard residents, as in Ballymacarrett, fought to repel attacks.

Women with babies fled along Cupar Street as gunfire, including a Lewis machine-gun, showed no compassion in its indiscriminate bearing on the people.

As in east Belfast, the military showed no favouritism on who they directed their fire against. Five of those killed by the military between the periods of 21st July-25th July in the Falls/Shankill Road interjection, were from a Protestant/Unionist background, including two former WW1 veterans.

Seven Catholics also died during the same period in West Belfast, including two former soldiers.

That day, [22nd July] in Belfast, twelve people died and forty-six were wounded.

The reign of terror left a pathetic sight of many homeless people wandering the streets looking for shelter.

Small handcarts were used to salvage belongings. In many cases, whole families were affected, the situation made worst by the cries of distressed children.

With a feeling of dispirit, they sought shelter wherever they could find it.

This was a time of poverty and survival, with no welfare state to draw support from.

They were in fact refugees in their own city.

Church halls and relatives were the only option open to them, in what were already overcrowded, cramped small terrace houses.

Many of these already accommodated large families and all this combined to the despair brought on by the attempted pogrom against Nationalist districts in Belfast.

Many families found themselves immigrating across to Glasgow, or Liverpool.

Former Ballymacarrett IRA Volunteer, Billy Murray recorded in his private papers:

"For the first few weeks of the riots it was a pitiful sight to stand in Seaforde Street and see these families coming in from the outside area looking for some place to shelter. When Catholic families fled, the mob went into the house, took everything out and piled it in the street and then set fire to it."

The military in their response, favoured no one. Of the ten people killed in Ballymacarrett in July and August of 1920, nine were Protestant, seven of whom were shot by the military, four of which were women, including a fifteen-year-old, shot during the disturbances around the Convent in Bryson Street on the 22nd July.

They also killed a Nationalist resident, Francis Mc Cann when firing into Seaforde Street at the end of August and wounded several others, during a confrontation between Nationalists and Shipyard workers who attempted to attack the Seaforde Street area.

Later, after the creation of the Special Constabulary, a Unionist state militia, a favourite tactic of this force in Belfast, was to deliberately open fire during curfew hours with the purpose of causing a reaction from the British military, who would then direct gunfire into the Nationalist streets which were tightly bound with small kitchen houses.

There was also the danger of gas pipes being punctured which could cause lung poisoning.

In his private papers, IRA Volunteer, Billy Murray, recorded several such incidents while on picket duty in Ballymacarrett during 1921.

Against this growing tide of attacks, the IRA decided to recruit and create a 2nd Battalion within Belfast to protect Nationalist districts.

Manus O'Boyle, a Donegal man working in the Short Strand area of Belfast and an IRA officer, set about recruiting local men in the Ballymacarrett/Short Strand district, being helped in this task by a local former British soldier, John-[Sean] Cunningham from Comber Street.

John Cunningham became the Company 2/IC-[2nd in command] and would later command the Company through 1921/22 amid the worst periods of conflict in Belfast.

Manus O'Boyle later recorded:

"I know the heaviest fighting took place in the Ballymacarrett area, where there were about 7,000 Catholics.

I was detailed then by the Brigade to organise a Company of volunteers for the defence of Ballymacarrett.

I succeeded in forming a Company of about 120 men. They were all unemployed.

Then the fighting proper commenced as we were now armed with small arms and grenades.

It was a continuous fight in Ballymacarrett. Our opponents were heavily armed and had the assistance of the Police and Military.

This continued all through 1920 and up until the truce"

Manus O'Boyle taken in later years in his home village of MountCharles Co Donegal. [Sean O'Coinn]

Billy Murray recorded:

"Manus O'Boyle regulated a small number of volunteers [around the Convent area] along with a few men who volunteered to help. They were split into two sections for pickets at different times during the night and for different nights during the week.

All these men were armed. James Faloona, John Cunningham and I stood picket duty every night for three weeks without relief.

We were armed and had plenty of small arms ammunition.

When the new picketing regulations came into operation, it was much better.

The district was divided into section areas and each Section Commander mobilised and regulated his own pickets. All arms and collections; everything pertaining toward control and discipline in the district was under the authority of the IRA."

Billy recalled the last *major* attack of 1920 against St. Matthew's towards the end of that summer. It occurred on a Wednesday afternoon about 3pm, when a large crowd of mainly young men attacked the church [This may have possibly been on the 26th August.]:

"The alarm was raised by some lads who were standing near the parochial hall and men from the surrounding streets rushed into the church grounds.

Women started to dig up kidney pavers and carry them around to the chapel grounds in their aprons. Some seized hand carts and filled them up and took them around to convenient places.

The men in the grounds charged out from behind the church and the mob fled in all directions.

A few men who had small arms including a policeman in civic clothes did not spare the ammunition on this occasion.

A large number of Catholic men who were armed with sticks, chased part of the mob down Frazer Street and Josephine Street, smashing most of the windows of the houses in those streets."

[Many decades later, in more recent times, history repeated itself several times in much the same vein as described by Billy in 1920, except that the kidney pavers were now bricks and bottles and the hand carts were replaced with wheelie bins!!]

The events of 1920 across Belfast was unfortunately only the beginning of what was to beset the city, from the Summer of 1921, when it escalated into a daily *"shooting war"* within the conflict areas on a scale no one could have imagined.

British Army, Lewis machine Gun post in Ballymacarrett, 1921

From the Spring of 1921, daily sniping had become commonplace around areas such as Ballymacarrett, Carrick Hill, the Marrowbone and York Street, while the IRA established a *"Squad"*, based in the centre of the city on the 1st floor of 5, Rosemary Street, primarily to strike at RIC, or Auxiliaries, passing through Belfast on short stays.

These actions were described by IRA officer Rodger Mc Corley, as *"Targets of opportunity"*.

Referring to Billy Murray's papers again, an interesting extract states that during this time, the Spring of 1921 that:

"The IRA succeeded in procuring a number of new rifles including some Lee Enfield's. It was easy getting ammunition at this time both from the police and military.

A number of men in B.Company - [Ballymacarrett, 2nd Battalion], went through the war in France and had nothing to learn about sniping. So these men put a sudden end to most of the Loyalist snipers who were terrorising the Catholic area [at that time]"

There were a number of men in B.Company - [Ballymacarrett/Short Strand] who had been in the British Army and served in the Great War.

The experience these men would have processed was invaluable.

Around the same period, the IRA in Belfast received German *Parabellums* [German made semi-automatic Lugar pistols].

Mary Mc Clean who was in Cumann Na mBan, recalled two cases of these weapons being brought to her home in Leeson Street for distribution to the volunteers.

After 18 months of intense guerrilla actions through-out Ireland, the Republican Leadership in Dublin announced on the 9th July that a ceasefire between republican forces and the British would come into effect at noon on Monday 11th July 1921.

But while the south of the country celebrated, Belfast bled!

On what became known as *"Bloody Sunday"* in Belfast, Nationalist districts came under sustained attack from several hundred regular and special police in Crossley tenders and Lancia armoured cars.

In Ballymacarrett, Volunteer Billy Murray of B.Company, recorded:

"On the day of the truce two men arrived back from Belgium and Paris loaded down with small arms such as Peter the Painters, Parabellums and Webley's and a good supply of ammunition to fit. These were welcome in this area.

For nights before the truce every man in B.Company and a host of men from the district remained ready armed with everything from bayonets to Lee Enfield rifles."

The weekend of the truce was ushered in with blood-letting as Unionist gunmen and, Specials began firing into Nationalist streets as the IRA mobilised to defend their areas.

Sixteen people died of whom eleven were Nationalist and 161 homes were destroyed. Gun-battles, involving machine-gun and rifle fire, as well as handguns and mills bombs were reported along the streets interlinking the Falls and Shankill Road.

Heavy fire was also reported in the Falls/Cullintree Road area, and the Millfield and Carrick Hill districts.

An IRA Volunteer, Paddy Burns of Carrick Hill recounted:

"The shooting went on all day and for up to 12 hours"

Carrick Hill was close to running out of ammunition and Rodger Mc Corley of the Brigade Staff stated:

"We couldn't get through to help, but we did manage to get the military to intervene and implement the truce."

It should be stressed that in Belfast, unlike in the south, the IRA seldom targeted British military personnel in its operations, as the *"enemy"*, was more the *"Specials"* who waged war on the Nationalist community in a blatant sectarian manner.

The British military seemed content to respect the truce in the initial stages, but the Specials who were acting as the armed wing of the new Northern administration, which had been officially constituted by the British King in June 1921, continued to act against the Nationalist areas with the full endorsement of the Belfast Parliament.

British soldiers manning a barricade in Belfast 1921.
The Cashman Collection

The IRA in Belfast were operating in a hostile environment flooded with British troops, Police and Specials who targeted the Nationalist/Catholic community in acts of reprisals which stretched from merely shooting into Catholic streets during the curfew hours, to conducting actual murder.

Added to this was the poor social condition in the Catholic working-class districts which was caused in part by expulsions from employment and also the overcrowding due to relatives and friends being forced out of their homes in Protestant/Unionist areas.

The IRA now found themselves primarily engaged in a defensive role, *to the best of their ability*, of the Nationalist districts, while still attempting to be *"offensive"* against the Specials and Unionist gunmen.

The whole mood of political uncertainty around the terms of the truce was the signal for a renewed wave of *bloody violence* at the end of August 1921, during which 21 people lost their lives over a three-day period.

The worst of the fighting was centred on the Nationalist side of York Street. The attacks on this district were planned to clear out the Nationalist streets and send a message to Britain that no settlement involving the IRA, was possible in the new state of Northern Ireland, which comprised the six north-eastern counties of the country, which held a Unionist majority.

However, the IRA was mobilised to defend the area, and that broke the gunmen's siege.

Seven Protestants were killed and the *Manchester Guardian* reported that the IRA:

> "Was retaliating in kind and quite as effectively as the Loyalist gunmen".

The IRA also possessed a large number of Mills grenades and had received further arms from the south and was well stocked with rifles.

But they were still greatly out-numbered and had a strong military and economic establishment against them, while in the south; a civil war loomed within republicans over the terms of the treaty. At that time, republicans would only have made up no more than 25% of the population of Belfast.

The autumn and winter's months marked an increase in shootings across the Nationalist districts and by the end of 1921, 109 people had died.

Belfast found itself embroiled in full sectarian warfare.

During the week period of 19th-25th November, 1921, 27 people were killed and 92 injured across the city and December fared no better.

Another development of the increasing sectarian nature that had been forced into the fighting was IRA attacks on shipyard trams carrying workers to and back from the Belfast Shipyard from were Catholic workers had been forcefully expelled, including Catholic WW1 veterans in July 1920.

It was seen as a way of *"hitting back"* and at the end of November; two trams were attacked with Mills bombs, killing two passengers in each of the attacks.

Other trams would be fired at as they passed areas such as Ballymacarrett/Short Strand, were heavy gun-battles were now a frequent occurrence as the area was constantly under attack from all ends.

Numerous raids by the military and Specials into the Nationalist district followed these gun-battles, searching for weapons, despite the IRA being engaged in a defensive role.

The *East-end*, was now described in the local press as *"The most dangerous place in Belfast"*.

As the ferocity of the conflict escalated through-out the spring of 1922, Unionist attacks increased on Nationalist districts around York Street, the Docks area and the Marrowbone district in the north of the city.

The IRA responded by attacking Specials, but this often resulted in reprisals against innocent Catholics and age or gender mattered little to the gunmen.

The worst of the killing came in April and May of 1922 with an upsurge of shooting, bombing, arson and intimidation. During May, there were 75 deaths - [42 Catholics and 33 Protestants] as Belfast descended into the *bloody climax* of the conflict.

Upwards of two hundred Catholic families were forced from their homes in north Belfast and many headed south to Dublin seeking refuge, or crossed the Irish Sea to Glasgow.

In the Marrowbone, Antigua and Sanderson Streets were burned out and pleas for help from the Belfast Protection Society on the plight of the Nationalist community, met with little practical help.

Ballymacarrett, the Marrowbone, Ardoyne and the Market districts came in for an onslaught over the weekend of 20th-21st May.

Raids were carried out by a force of Military, Police and Specials in the Short Strand searching for weapons on Thursday, 18th May, despite heavy firing into the Short Strand from Unionist snipers.

Constant sniping occurred around the lower end of the Newtownards Road throughout the afternoon of Saturday 20th, beginning at 3.30pm in the afternoon, and continued the following lunch-time, with snipers firing around Bridge End and Short Strand.

In the Marrowbone and Ardoyne to the north of the city, the residents were subjected to a week of machine-gun and rifle fire by the Specials for two hours each night until curfew hours - [10pm to 6am].

They would advance from their base in extended order to the fields at the back of Ardoyne and generally around 8.45pm, assume prone firing positions and direct gunfire down into the streets.

As the weekend came to a close on Sunday 21st May, the Market district suffered from a regular attack by Specials on foot and in cage cars.

From the safe distance of the Gas Works and the old Slaughter House, they were observed lying on the streets firing into the houses, as people were forced to lie on the floors avoiding the windows as everybody and everything, became a target.

However, it was the week commencing on Monday 22nd May, 1922, that was to prove a defining turning point and would mark an event that would become a trademark of the Northern Administration for the next fifty years.

Monday 22nd May, 1922 will not be remembered or recorded in the annals of the conflict for the daily cross-divide sniping around the Short Strand which left two Protestants killed and two Specials wounded on the Albert Bridge.

Or, for two Catholic men killed in the north of the city; this was the norm for Belfast!

The news however was focused primarily on an incident that had sent shock waves through the Unionist hierarchy, when that morning, William Twaddell, a member of the Northern Parliament and leader of the Ulster Imperial Guard, an organization made up of

RIC at Kent Street and Royal Avenue, outside Belfast Library, 1922.

Unionist WW1 veterans, was shot and killed by two gunmen as he walked along Lower Garfield Street toward his Drapery business premises at 59 Lower North Street, in the centre of Belfast.

William Twaddell was an outspoken Loyalist and the UIG membership also consisted of many Specials. They were also involved in attacks on Nationalist districts; one of their members being killed during a gun-battle in Ballymacarrett over the week-end of 17th/18th December, 1921, shot by a B.Company sniper from Young's Row.

The two men involved in the shooting of Twaddell made their escape through Smithfield into a Nationalist district and came from the 2nd Battalion's C.Company.

Whether or not, the shooting was authorised by the Brigade Staff, or an independent shooting, is open to question, but the consequence of it, marked a defining point in the conflict of that period.

The shooting of William Twaddell and the IRA burning of Unionist owned business premises in the centre of Belfast, was to mark the introduction of Internment by the northern administration.

The introduction of Internment saw a large concentration of Military, Police, and Specials move against Nationalist districts on Tuesday morning, 23rd May, at 04.00am. They were backed by armoured cars and the initial raids within Belfast resulted in 39 men being arrested.

The men arrested were conveyed to Chichester Street police cells for a 24-hour holding period.

That evening a strong force of Police and Specials attacked Carrick Hill and the IRA replied with whatever they had at their disposal. The gunfire extended down into North Street and Kent Street into the top end of Royal Avenue.

The IRA intentionally fired down into the centre, bringing the fight to the heart of Belfast which was decorated for *"Empire Day"*, Wednesday the 24th.

The following day, Wednesday, the normally busy town was quiet as a convoy of cage cars and their escort of armoured cars, made its way up North Street toward the Old Lodge Road in the direction of Crumlin Road Gaol.

The prisoners were handcuffed in threes; six prisoners in each cage car with a Special standing in each corner with a rifle at the ready.

Billy Murray, who was one of the prisoners, recorded the journey in his papers:

> *"The Specials in the cage car in which I was, kept singing all the way from Chichester Street until we reached the prison; Kevin Barry you're a Bastard, you're a dirty Fenian Bastard, and while singing this, kept looking sideways at us prisoners.*
>
> *They kept their rifles pointed at us, or sometimes over the side of the cage car.*
>
> *As we passed California Street and into a Loyalist area, a mob of screaming people of all ages and sexes, threw muck and small stones at us."*

As Billy Murray and other prisoners, some from his own area of Ballymacarrett, were being driven into Internment at the Gaol, the shooting continued.

A tram carrying Protestant workers travelling through the Nationalist side of the Mountpottinger Road in the Short Strand was fired upon and in a separate incident in the same area, B.Company threw a mills bomb at a patrol wounding a Special; Constable Hanna.

The previous evening at around 9pm, three bombs were thrown into the East Yard of the Sirocco Works on the Mountpottinger Road as the Specials were billeted there.

While the shooting continued across the city, Billy Murray and the other Internees were put on to B.3 and given eight ounces of bread. Billy described his first night in Gaol *as a strange experience*, lying on the narrow hard bed on the floor; he spent it listening to the rifle, machine-gun and revolver fire, which lasted well after midnight.

That first night is one of thought, of reflection of the day's events, of family and the question of what was to come next!

The next morning the prisoners were let out into a small yard, which they later knew as being C.Wing yard. When the Internees refused to walk in single file as with ordinary non-political prisoners, a dispute broke out and the men stood around in groups discussing their next move.

The stalemate was suddenly broken, when C.Wing yard's gate opened and to the amazement of the Belfast Internees, a large crowd of men began to file into the yard, which completely dwarfed the dispute.

Billy Murray stated:

> *"Country men from all over the six counties, except Derry men, of all stations of life; Doctors, Solicitors, Vet nary Surgeons, Farmers, Shop Keepers of all kinds, Labourers, and Tradesmen.*
>
> *Most of the farmers and labourers had their working clothes on. Some were arrested at work in the fields, others from behind shop counters, or taken from behind the wheel of a car, or lorry that they were driving.*
>
> *From Tyrone, Fermanagh, Armagh, there were men wearing all shapes of hats and clothes of ancient and modern styles."*

So here was the scene on the first day of Internment in Crumlin Road Gaol in May 1922, described by one of those in the yard that morning of Thursday, 25th May.

For the first three or four days, the men simply congregated in small groups in the C.Wing yard. The weather was good, but there was little space for exercise.

They started Irish classes and the *Angelus* was said each day.

A Commandant was elected, Dr. Jim Mc Kee from Banbridge.

He became the first Internees Commandant in Crumlin Road Gaol, under the new Northern State., during this initial short stay, which lasted until Tuesday night, 22nd June, when the Internees were told to pack up for moving to the Prison Ship *Argenta.*

One event that is important to record in this book is the eye-witness account of the attack on the Mater Hospital from within the Gaol by the B.Specials, a platoon of whom were billeted in the prison hospital on guard detail.

Billy Murray recorded the following:

"On the 4th June-[1922], I witnessed the start of the attack on the Mater hospital. It was just about dusk and I was standing on a small table looking out of my window in B.3. I had a clear view of the prison hospital.

I noticed a Special walking fast toward the hospital door. Then he suddenly stopped, drew his revolver and discharged it into the air.

Then running toward the [hospital] door, he shouted: Guard turn out.

Then I saw this platoon rush out carrying rifles and a machine-gun and run down the yard out of sight.

The Internees on the other side of B.3 saw these men running toward the Wood yard, where they had a clear view of the rear and west wing of the Mater hospital.

From here they began firing up at the hospital."

Patients on the wards facing out on to the Gaol, which included several policemen, wounded in the recent day's shootings, had to throw mattresses against the windows and lie on the ground as bullets perforated the walls and windows.

When the hospital authorities contacted the Police and Military, they were told that the IRA were using the hospital roof to attack the Gaol, which was a total fabrication.

The Gaol hospital, August 2008. Note the V.R and Crown, 1898 above the entrance [Author]

Conditions on the *Argenta* were cramped, crude and extremely poor and men were prone to falling ill at times. Some of the Internees were former soldiers who had fought in WW1 and were suffering from TB and Asthma as a result of hardships incurred in France.

Fresh air was not in great supply and bedding consisted of a narrow mattress fitted with soft meadow hay, three old army blankets, with a life belt for a pillow.

The Medical Officer paid very little attention to any complaints and each cage housed an average of forty men in cramped conditions.

The story of the *Argenta* is for another book.

Billy Murray, would, like others on the ship, suffer health issues and before his release from Internment in June 1924, he would also spend time in Derry Gaol and another period back in the *"Crumlin Road"* to recover from health issues.

Unfortunately, for him when he walked through the gates of the Gaol that warm sunny day back in June 1924, it was not to be the end of his association with *"The Crum"*.

The outbreak of the civil war on the 27th June, 1922 in the south over the terms of the treaty, and the death of Michael Collins, in August, proved to be the *"Death Nail"* for the Northern IRA. It became the policy of the new Free State Government, *Cumann Na nGaedheal*, to absorb the Northern IRA into the Free State Army.

An Armoured Car in Royal Avenue 1922

While Michael Collins was genuine in his efforts to support the north and create a policy of direction for the Northern Divisions, others within the Provisional government, such as Ernest Blythe and Kevin O'Higgins, were pursuing a different agenda.

At that time, 379 volunteers from the Northern Divisions were at the Curragh camp under a so-called training scheme for further action in Belfast and the north.

The defeat of the Anti-Treaty Republican forces in the civil war, and the policy of recognition of the northern state by the Cumann Na nGaedheal government in Dublin led by William Cosgrave, cemented partition and led to the end of the Northern Divisions.

The 3rd Northern Division which covered Belfast was officially disbanded on the 31st March, 1923, leaving volunteers to either join the Free State Army, or simply *"Go home".*

Following the *"Dump Arms"* order of the 24th" May, 1923, a complete re-organization of the IRA began under Chief of Staff, Frank Aiken from Camlough in South Armagh.

Sinn Fein, now under the leadership of Eamon Donnelly, returned 44 Abstentionist Candidates in the *Dail* in 1924, rising to 48, due to By-Elections.

In the north and in Belfast, the IRA was in a poor state and needed to completely reform and re-build; many volunteers were now in the Free State Army including experienced officers. Others were forced to emigrate due to unemployment within a hostile state, or were expelled to England.

Republicans in Belfast and other areas were regularly arrested and harassed and there was a deliberate agenda on the part of the northern administration to discourage republicans who had joined the Free State Army from returning to the north, although many did.

For those that remained, training and re-organization began slowly, spearheaded by the release of the Internees in 1924, although many of them were served with *"Expulsion Orders"* from the six-counties.

In some areas, training was conducted under the guise of Gaelic Athletic Clubs, as the aim of reforming the Belfast Battalion-[Not

Brigade], was underway under Hugh Corvin, a former Brigade officer.

One of the first meetings took place in a room above a small bookshop on the corner of Marquis Street and Castle Street to resurrect D.Company, which covered the Divis/Pound Loney area.

Arms dumps were sought out in districts such as Ballymacarrett / Short Strand, North Queen Street and Divis to be lifted, or re-activated.

B.Company was to cover- Ballymacarrett; C.Company was to cover North Belfast and D.Company the Falls District.

Despite state persecution, the IRA was functioning again, *even if at an all-time low.*

Republican Prisoners after their release from Crumlin Road Gaol.

Raids and arrests continued. The Short Strand in particular was raided numerous times.

On the 11th August, 1923, the RUC acting on information received, discovered a haul of ammunition at the Anderson Felt Works. This find was the first of three to be uncovered at the same location between August 1923 and January 1925.

All of the material dated back to the 1920-22 period and had remained undetected during that crucial period of fighting.

Again in the Short Strand, a force of RUC and Specials raided into the district on the night of 18th September, 1924 and the RUC from Mountpottinger Barracks, under District Inspector Spears were once more called to the Anderson Felt Works by the manager, who told them that ammunition and six mills bombs had been discovered in a store.

A .303 Lee Enfield rifle was also discovered the following morning.

Follow up raids were made in the district. An RUC REPORT from the Commissioner's Office stated that:

"Raids took place in the Sinn Fein area of the district, where it was thought further arms might be found, but without success. These arms are the property of the local IRA and as no local rebels could be connected with this find, no arrests were made."

During the conflict period of 1920-22, despite numerous raids in that area by the military, RIC and Specials, weapons dumps, in the main, remained undetected.

There were a few finds uncovered such as in Seaforde Street in October 1922 and Foundry Street, but this was at the end of the conflict period, and were not any significant finds, such as rifles.

Two main dumps during that period remained un-detected.

However, as raids continued, arrests were made and republicans once more found themselves back on the wings of Crumlin Road Gaol.

William Devlin of Vulcan Street was charged with possession of a pistol and ammunition in 1924.

The following year, John Connolly of Thompson Street, Joseph Mc Clenland of Anderson Street, John Walsh and Dan Mc Gurk of Chemical Street, all from the Short Strand area, were charged at various dates during 1925.

John Walsh was charged in August 1925 with possession of explosives, arms and ammunition and the following month, Joe Mc Gurk was charged under the **Special Powers Act**, with membership of an *"unlawful association"* and having illegal documents.

Joe Mc Gurk was sentenced to three months in Crumlin Road Gaol, having refused to recognise the court. [Joe was again sentenced in 1933 for addressing a banned Easter parade in Co. Tyrone and was interned in December 1938.]

John Walsh's term of imprisonment would have been much severe.

Under the Special Powers Act, so-called seditious documents could include a copy of the republican paper, *An Phoblact*, or even a copy of the 1916 Proclamation.

Examples of these draconian measures in suppressing anything of a republican nature can be found in the Magistrate's Court on 30th December 1937:

Sergeant Wilson, RUC told a court of searching a club in Beechfield Street, in the Short Strand area, and discovering there;

"examination papers in Irish, with a series of questions relating to republicanism".

D.I Geelan, RUC, corroborated. Constable Peters gave evidence of:

"finding in the club upon Denis Whelan, the script of a play, derogatory of the Special Constabulary".

D.I Hamilton, RUC charged republican Peter Fanning [An IRA man from the twenties period] from the Springfield Road, with being in possession of a copy of the 1916 Proclamation, *such a document*, said the Inspector, *"Being likely to cause disaffection"*.

It had been seized during a raid on the Wolfe Tone Republican Club- [Pearse Hall] in King Street, used widely by republicans in the thirties and known for its great *Ceilis*.

Even the wearing of an Easter *Lilly*, could evoke a month in Crumlin Road Gaol.

At the same court, nine men, around 18 years of age, had sentences imposed on them for taking part in a commemoration in Milltown cemetery for Joe Mc Kelvey, executed by Free State Forces during the civil war.

The parade was warned by Sergeant Fanning that their assembly was unlawful and with a force of 50 armed RUC men, moved in to arrest the offenders.

Daniel Doherty, from Sheriff Street, Ballymacarrett, who gave commands in Irish; Felix Kelly, Chemical Street, Ballymacarrett, Alex Mc Atamney, Fleet Street, John O'Connor, Nelson Street, both from the Docks area, and John Campbell, Jamaica Street, Ardoyne; were all given six months imprisonment in Crumlin Road Gaol, while Patrick Ferran, of Parkview Street and Daniel Mc Allister of Lincoln Street, were both sentenced to one month's imprisonment, for wearing illegal emblems.

Denis Whelan, of Bridge End, Ballymacarrett was sentenced to one year imprisonment in his absence.

[Daniel Doherty, who was a member of the Fianna and later the IRA in Ballymacarrett, became a fluent Irish speaker, *"Gaelgoir"* and for many years of his life promoted the teaching of the language. He was interned in Crumlin Road Gaol in the forties period]

Such an occurrence is unthinkable today, or during the recent conflict, but this was 1937, 85 years ago!

As the IRA attempted to re-build during the late twenties, raids on Nationalist districts continued.

In 1926, Jim Johnston from Tyrone Street in Carrick Hill was arrested for possession of weapons; George Nash of 52 Gibson Street, a well-known republican, was arrested in June 1928 also due to an arms find.

The same year, a raid uncovered: Fifteen Service rifles, five Martini rifles, eleven pistols, one Thompson sub-machine-gun, thirty-one grenades, at 17 Linden Street in the Falls Road district. This would have been a huge blow to an IRA in the middle of a re-building process.

Despite these setbacks, the IRA continued to grow and recruit in Belfast.

Bob Bradshaw from the Falls district joined the *Fianna* in 1925, aged twelve. Two years later, having turned fourteen, he went up to the *Mc Kelvey* hut, a small timber structure at Rockmore Street near the Whiterock Road which acted as a Belfast HQ for the IRA, seeking to move into the IRA.

Tony Lavery, the O.C took one look at him and said:

"Come back Son, when you are out of short pants", leaving young Bob deflated.

But not to be deterred, Bob presented himself back at the *Mc Kelvey* hut a year later, wearing long pants, and Davy Matthews *took him on.*

Jack Brady from Kilmood Street joined the IRA through the Fianna in Ballymacarrett.

At 19 years of age, he was a Staff officer, and at 25, he was interned on the *Al Rawdah* Prison Ship in 1940.

Jim Stranney and Willie O' Hanlon from the Short Strand district, both joined from the Fianna, and were in the Ballymacarrett Company, when Jack Brady was the O.C of the district in 1935.

Both men later fought in Spain during the civil war with the XV International Brigade, Jim Stranney being killed at the Ebro in August 1938.

On the broad political front, as in 1922, politics in the south had a direct bearing on the position of republicans in the north.

Following the Sinn Fein *Ard Fheis* of the 9th March, 1926, Eamon de Valera resigned as President of Sinn Fein, due to a difference of policy and direction.

A few weeks later, De Valera announced the formation of a new political party called *Fianna Fail* [Republican Party]. It was officially launched at the La Scala theatre on Prince's Street in Dublin on the 26th May, 1926, with De Valera elected as President.

Still using republican rhetoric of standing for an all- Ireland Republic and the need to end partition, De Valera addressed rallies all over the country, even bringing his message to the United States on two fund raising trips.

When Fianna Fail branches sprang up all over the 26 counties, De Valera was making off with Sinn Fein's republican emotional baggage.

Following victory in the election of March 1932, Fianna Fail entered the Dail and Eamon de Valera was once more the President of Ireland.

Nine years after their defeat in the civil war, a *"Republican Party"* was again in power in the Free State. Those who carried the mantle of the anti-treaty forces during the civil war had now turned military defeat into political victory.

Political prisoners were released and republicans throughout Ireland celebrated.

Throughout the thirties, De Valera undid most of what republicans felt to be unacceptable in the 1921 treaty.

However, if republicans in the north felt that deliverance was at hand, those hopes were soon shattered, as Fianna Fail, although still professing itself as a republican party, moved away from the concept of armed struggle, and having used the IRA to gain power, now proscribed it.

De Valera split the Republican Movement by offering pensions and appointments in what was a twenty-six county state, not an all-Ireland Irish Republic.

Those who accepted, entered the establishment and just as in 1922, those who remained loyal to the Republic, were outlawed and persecuted.

De Valera contributed greatly in tearing apart the IRA at a time in the early 1930's, when it had regained its strength following the civil war. He took away its political soul, in order to pursue *"his political aims"*.

His actions contributed in cementing partition, the very thing he pledged to dismantle in his political rhetoric.

His government broke the strength of the IRA in the south by enticing republicans into a Free State Army in order to isolate *"Militant Republicanism"*.

Military tribunals were re-established on the 22nd August, 1933 and in November of the same year, a new volunteer force was established, [today's FCA-Army Reserve], all designed to break up the IRA.

Republicanism was now more a tool of traditional propaganda, than any move, militant or otherwise, toward unification.

Men such as the hard-line Frank Aiken, from South Armagh, entered the establishment and he became the new Minister of Defence, strongly opposing IRA activity.

Gerard Boland, who hailed from a strong republican background [and who was the brother of Harry Boland, a, close friend of Michael Collins, killed in the civil war by Free State troops], later became Minister for Justice and implemented an extreme hard-line policy against republicans brought before his "special courts".

His draconian measures ranged from military courts to the execution of republicans, emulating on a smaller scale his predicators of Cumann na nGaedhead.

Gerard Boland was typical of the new Fianna Fail administration at the time.

When we look today at the recent conflict and the peace agreement that developed from it, it is clear to see how history, particularly Irish history has a tendency, *to repeat itself.*

The reality is that every conflict has to have a political end-game, and often the key players of that conflict become key elements of the political system that evolves from peace.

Frank Aiken and Martin Mc Guinness, very alike in their republican credentials, in different periods of history, are two good examples of the political end-game.

Both were considered hard-line in conflict; both entered the establishment in peace taking ministerial roles and both moved away from militant republicanism.

Stability in any political system takes preference over old loyalties, it is a harsh reality. It does not necessarily justify, or excuse it, but there is nothing romantic about conflict and in the end, politics will always end up as the dominating factor of the two.

Unfortunately, there is also the double edged sword *for some* of careers taking preference over principles and too often in contemporary Irish history, core principles have been sacrificed.

Due to an increase in sporadic shootings and bombings by the IRA during the thirties, the Northern Parliament again turned to Internment at the end of 1938.

Events on the ground, although largely insignificant by the standards of the recent conflict, were enough to lay its preparation. In Dublin, a similar policy was implemented, inevitably *"closing the safe ground"*.

Three days before Christmas 1938 on Thursday, 22nd December, dawn raids by the RUC and Specials were made in the Falls, Ballymacarrett, Ardoyne, and York Street districts. The initial arrests amounted to 34 men being detained under the Special Powers Act and despatched to Crumlin Road Gaol.

Among those detained in Ballymacarrett was Billy Murray!

Although no longer a member of the IRA, "He had a past and was still a republican".

That was enough to be arrested and interned.

Billy himself, also believed that his assistance to a fellow republican in Ballymacarrett in collecting money to help the families of republican prisoners in the district coming up to Christmas, may also have been a factor in his arrest as they were being observed for two days by several RUC detectives from Mountpottinger Barracks.

Billy accounted the morning Internment was introduced for the second time by the northern administration:

"On Thursday morning about 04:30am, I was awakened by loud hammering on my front door and ongoing down was surprised to see a District Inspector, Head Constable and several police

waiting to be admitted. A search of the house was carried out, but nothing of importance was found.

I was told to get dressed and landed up in Mountpottinger Barracks, to find four other men including the chum that I was collecting with, sitting there also. None of us knew this was a round up for Internment.

About 05.30am, we were removed to Chichester Street Police Barrack. There were twenty-nine other men, making a party of thirty-four. That evening we were conveyed to Crumlin Road prison.

On Friday, all the Belfast newspapers carried large headlines "ROUND UP OF IRA LEADERS IN BELFAST". The minister for Home Affairs-[Dawson Bates] told the press that the police authorities had discovered a plot, and that the government decided to arrest and intern these thirty-four leaders.

Now of these thirty-four leaders; seven were not connected to any organisation, eighteen were just volunteers, leaving eighteen who could be IRA officers."

We can account for two of the Ballymacarrett men arrested that morning with Billy; they were: Joe Boales, and Arthur Mullen, both of Seaforde Street.

Billy and the rest of the Internees were housed on D.1 and the following morning, just as in 1922, a dispute began as the men refused to walk in single file as with ordinary criminals. After some debate, the Governor relented and they walked to their own manner.

On a cold snowy Christmas Day, Billy recalled the sentenced republican prisoners on A.Wing gave them cake, confectionary and cigarettes as they had no parcels as yet.

On the 5th January, 1939, they were called in one at a time by two Detectives from Chichester Street and given out Internment Orders.

These were mostly *torn up* and they stood and sang the National Anthem.

Following this, the men demanded Internees treatment and elected Sean Mc Nally of Ardilea Street as their O.C and Jim Nolan, from Mc Cleery Street as Adjutant.

Thus began the second period of Internment in Crumlin Road Gaol.

As in the 1922-1923 periods, Billy along with many more of the growing number of Internees, would find himself back in Derry Gaol; another prison ship, this time the SS *AL RAWDAH*, before returning to *Crumlin Road* until his release in July 1945.

Others escaped the initial Internment swoop having volunteered to cross to England to carry out bombings. This was probably the *"Plot"*, Dawson Bares referred to, not knowing the precise nature of it and assuming it was to be in the north.

Albert Price, Gerry Kerr, Frankie Duffy, Albert Mc Nally, Maggie Nolan, Dominic Adams, Harry White and Jimmy Mc Gowan had left for England, to embark on a campaign that lacked any real strategy. [Other volunteers would follow]

The IRA where not concerned with the material damage, but more the psychological effect brought about by random attacks. They did not have the logistics at that time, or the purpose to damage the British transportation structure; it was more intended to maintain the momentum of incidents.

The English Bombing Campaign resulted in 200 small explosions, resulting in scores of IRA volunteers being imprisoned, two executed on the 7th February, 1940 at Winston Green Prison in Birmingham-[Peter Barnes and Jimmy Mc Cormack] and three dying in prison.

The Easter parade of 1939 commemorating the 1916 rising was banned by the northern administration in Stormont.

Not to be denied some kind of acknowledgment of this most important date in republican folklore, republicans marched on Easter Saturday in the Short Strand, Marrowbone and Falls Road district to the homes of three volunteers who were killed during the 1920-22 periods, were a statement from the IRA was read out.

In the Short Strand they walked from Anderson Street to number 5 Moira Street, home of Volunteer Murtagh Mc Astocker, killed in September 1921; In the Marrowbone, they walked to Mayfair Street to the home of Volunteer David Morrison killed in December 1921, and in the Falls, they walked to Cyprus Street, to the home of Joe Mc Kelvey, executed by the Free State in 1922.

Charges were brought against twenty-five men and women for wearing Easter lilies.

Mary Donnelly, May Laverty, Bridget Corr, Felix Kelly, Robert Donaldson, Helen Hayes, Mary Mc Mahon, Sarah Jane Mc Cartney, Winnie Simmington, Kathleen Quinn, Jean Ryan, Phil Mc McCullough and Barney Boswell.

[Robert Donaldson of Anderson Street would be arrested the following year after raids into the Short Strand and weapons being discovered. He was sentenced to ten years imprisonment in Crumlin Road Gaol. Felix Kelly, of Chemical Street, Ballymacarrett/Short Strand was interned on the *Al Rawdah* as was Barney Boswell of New Andrew Street in the Docks area.]

In October 1939, further raids in Belfast brought thirty-nine more men into the Gaol, which included Seamus *"Rocky"* Burns, Liam Burke, Jimmy Drumn, Paddy Morrison and Jack Mc Clusky.

Just as life had settled down for the Internees in Crumlin Road Gaol, speculation was rife of an intended move to Derry.

On Halloween night, 31st October, 1939, the Ballymacarrett Internees gathered in a cell on D.2 and had themselves a little tea party from their parcels, and as Billy Murray stated" *The first drop of good tea, some of us had since being arrested."*

However, eleven days later, on Friday morning, 10th November, 1939, the Internees found themselves en route from Belfast to Derry Gaol.

Taken in convoy, with several tenders of police to the front and rear, they arrived in Derry at 1pm and were housed in the top tier of the old prison.

Food was good in Derry and conditions were much improved since 1922 and regular parcels came into the Gaol, but this did not prevent a *"Prisoners Mutiny"* at Christmas to highlight their plight of Internment by a state, which was now at war with Germany.

The *mutiny* was suppressed by bringing in the RUC and Specials armed with rifles, backed by the Military and the Derry Fire Brigade who hosed the tier from both ends.

The republican O.C of the Gaol, Sean Mc Ardle was beaten by a number of Specials with the butts of their rifles. Many internees had head wounds and the Firemen threw buckets of water over men as they lay injured.

They achieved their objective of highlighting their internment, but with little positive results for the men themselves.

The year 1940, was one of *ebb and flow* for republican activity.

The most important event was a daring raid on the armoury of Ballykinlar camp in February, which netted thirty Lee Enfield rifles.

Raids quickly followed against the usual Nationalist districts in a bid to try and recover the weapons.

In April 1940, the IRA organized Easter parades, although banned on *"Good Friday"* in the Ballymacarrett/Short Strand, Falls Road, Marrowbone and North Queen Street areas.

The same month, Volunteer Sean Martin died as a result of an explosion, when he sheltered comrades from a grenade, which when the pin was pulled, turned out to be *"live"* during a weapons class being held at 67 Anderson Street in the Short Strand.

William Mc Connell, in whose home the training lecture was taking place, was Gaoled in *Crumlin Road* for allowing his home to be used by the IRA. He was a republican from the 1920-22 periods.

The following month, republicans organized a march in the Falls Road against the possible introduction of conscription for the armed forces.

James Regan, of 1a Beechfield Street in the Short Strand was later charged and imprisoned in *Crumlin Road* for reading a statement at the rally.

The following month, June 1940, raids into the same district, unearthed five revolvers, a rifle, ammunition and documents.

Robert Donaldson, of 31 Anderson Street was later sentenced to ten years imprisonment in *Crumlin Road.*

On 1st September that year, the military took over guard duties in Derry Gaol re-enforcing the prisoners concern that they were being transferred to a *"Prison Ship"*

The following morning at 0.5.00, the Internees were told to *"pack up"* and after breakfast, [which included, for the first time, *bacon*!] they were put on to a fleet of nine buses with a strong military and RUC escort and driven to Ebrington Barracks from where they preceded to Coleraine, for the journey toward Belfast.

The military escort was withdrawn at Coleraine, but Crossley tenders with Specials and the RUC remained, around 250 in total.

The convoy arrived at the Unionist village of Killyleagh, in County Down, where the SS *Al Rawdah* was moored at a point where the tides met, making any escape attempt a dangerous course of action.

As the Internees were ferried across to the ship in small boats, the Captain who was observing from his bridge, demanded that handcuffs be removed from the men, nor would he allow the RUC to board his ship an order that brought cheers from the boarding Internees.

The Madonna painted in Crumlin Road Gaol by a Republican prisoner in the Forties. [Author].

Nine days later, on the 10th September, seventy-two more men arrived, bringing the total to 207 Internees. The RUC, backed by Specials had carried out large raids on the Market, Short Strand and

Ardoyne, arresting forty men, who were brought to *Crumlin Road*. Some of these men were then transferred to the *Al Rawdah*.

The residents of the Unionist North Down fishing village resented the presence of the ship and the security that came with it. They equally resented the relatives of the internees who came to visit the men.

The first thing that many of the men had to adopt to was sleeping in hammocks, something that was a novelty to a lot of men, and an experience that until they adopted to, was a bit of a torture to begin with.

The men, despite the cramped conditions were treated with full Internee Status.

The boredom was the main problem and keeping a regulated form of discipline.

Billy Murray recorded that mass attendance quickly decreased and that the standards set by republicans interned during 1922-1924 were lacking, epically regarding military discipline and classes on Irish history, although by October Irish language classes were commenced and, in some quarters, the reciting of the rosary also began again as it would have done in the twenties.

However, there was no lack of souvenir creation as the men continually stripped the 3 ply wood around them to make harps, crosses and shields.

The main low point of Internment on the *Al Rawdah*, was the death through illness of John Gaffney on Monday morning, 18th November 1940.

Having taken ill in the early hours of that morning, he died in the little hospital on the No 2 Deck. At 5.30pm that day, the Internees were formed up in four Companies and called to attention. A number of the men carried his remains in relays along the deck to the Forward part of the ship and down the gangway and placed them in the motorboat.

Two Companies followed the remains to the Forward end and stood to attention, the other two Companies remained at attention at the aft part of the ship.

It took twenty minutes for the motorboat to reach Killyleagh Pier, and then the O.C dismissed the parade, leaving all in a sombre mood.

A plaque made by Billy on the Al Rawdah Internment Ship, 1940.
[Malachy Murray]

The Stormont Minister of Home Affairs, Dawson Bates had issued instructions that an inquest would not be held under emergency regulations, just an enquiry.

This was a precaution in case any evidence detrimental to the Government or its officials on the ship would come before the public.

The fact that two hours elapsed from his illness was reported to the night guard, until the Doctor-[Doctor Sproule] arrived was excluded, as was the fact he had complained three times to the Doctor previous to his death, of sickness.

[Billy Murray Papers]

Doctor Sproule had worked hard all morning to try and revive John Gaffney and had done all that was possible for him to do.

According to a post mortem his death was caused by cerebral-haemorrhage.

On the Wednesday, about 2pm as his remains left St. John's church on the Falls Road, the Internees assembled in the little chapel on the ship and the rosary was recited, followed by a two-minute silence.

The Captain of the ship had the flag flown at half-mast in respect.

A large crowd of mourners followed the cortege along the Falls Road, where John Gaffney was buried in the Republican Plot in Milltown Cemetery.

As Christmas approached, the Internees were working hard making crosses and harps. The racks where the hammocks were stored were fast disappearing along with the plywood drawers and cupboards.

Complaints from the ship's authorities, met with little success.

Apparently, just before Christmas one evening as relatives were leaving with their craftwork, the Captain stood on the bridge and was heard to say:

"There goes half my F....ing ship."

Christmas 1940 on the *Al Rawdah* was a good one as parcels from relatives had brought a fair amount of food in and the men organised a Christmas concert in the chapel.

Even the food from the ship on Christmas Day was good:

"Porridge, egg and bacon for Breakfast; with potato soup, roast turkey and ham, potatoes and cabbage for dinner."

The new year of 1941 brought cold and stormy weather and at the end of January, six of the Internees planned an escape attempt which had to be aborted when the alarm was raised.

Those involved were: Joseph O'Hagan, John-[Sean] Mc Ardle, Dan Dougherty, Billy Murray, Pat Toner and I Mc Naff.

Moral among the Internees was low and a state of despondency had set in when word came through that they were to be transferred back to Crumlin Road Gaol.

Relatives await a returning boat, to go on board the SS Al Rawdah, 1940

After five months on the *Al Rawdah*, in February 1941, the Internees returned to the *"Crum"*, which made visits much easier for relatives.

Upon arrival in the Gaol, the men found great changes since they left it for Derry back on the 10th November 1939.

The large workshop were convicted men used to work making mail bags, shoemaking etc. had been converted into a dining room, chapel, cookhouse and visiting box.

There were new dining tables, new mugs, plates and cutlery for each man.

They also found double bunks in each cell due to overcrowding and C.Wing, which now also had Internees, was full up due to continued raids being carried out, particularly the July 1940 raids.

In 1941, two major German air raids were carried out over Belfast in April and May.

For the prisoners and warders alike, it was a nerve wrecking experience.

Billy Murray was in cell 18 on D3 as not all of the Internees went to the shelter.

"We saw the flares and then the bombs began to fall. We watched the bombs exploding for about two hours, but the air pressure from the explosions was so terrific that we had to come away from the window. A large number of flares passed directly over the prison illuminating everything like daylight. Then a shower of incendiary bombs came down, some falling in the prison yard and a great number fell in St.Malachy's college grounds."

"Several times D.Wing rocked from the concussion of bombs dropped near-by."

"It certainly was a great relief to hear the siren signal the all-clear that morning at 0.5.00 am. I stood at my cell window

looking down over that vast furnace of flame and smoke; the burning smell was terrific".

The next day everything inside and outside of the Gaol was in a state of confusion as Belfast came to terms with the Luftwaffe raid.

Internees eagerly waited for news of relatives. One young man lost his mother and brother, and was released to identify them, despite a strong RUC objection, as he refused to sign any papers. However, the Governor allowed him to leave on his word of honour and was back inside the Gaol within a few hours.

Another Internee lost his sister, her husband and family.

One unexploded bomb lodged inside the tram lines opposite the courthouse and visits were suspended until it was removed. The water and gas supply into the Gaol was badly damaged and all water had to be boiled for cooking and drinking.

D. Wing - [End of Landing on D.3] Photo, June 2009. [Author]

In the second raid during May, all Internees were ordered to go to the shelter by the O.C and the rosary was recited several times during the night, especially when at one point during the raid the light failed in the shelter making it feel as if the Gaol had received a hit. A large mine did explode near the prison causing D.Wing to vibrate.

The following month, on Friday 5th June 1941, a sensation of a different nature went through the Gaol when five republicans managed to get through a ten feet corrugated iron fence which separated D.Wing from the wood yard and from there, they scaled the wall with a 12 foot rope made for the escape, into the grounds of St.Malachy's college.

The men: Liam Burke, Eddie Keenan, Phil Mc Taggart, Billy Watson and Gerry Doherty from Derry evaded the usual raids that followed and were quickly moved south to Dublin.

[Liam Burke would play a pivotal role in a number of actions during the forties period, including the successful escape of Republican prisoners from Derry Gaol in March 1943. He was re-arrested on Easter Sunday, 1943 along with Alphos White in a safe house in a Unionist area of south Belfast. A weapons cache was also captured.

On the 3rd August, 1943, a twelve-year sentence was imposed on both men by Lord Justice Murphy.

Following the escape, the fence was re-enforced and barbed wire entwined behind it. The RUC and Specials now patrolled the grounds of St.Malachy's college and the Internees movement had restrictions imposed on them.

Johnny Doherty, a young man in the Gaol from the Short Strand, remembered how when they were playing football, that if the ball went over the wall into the grounds of St.Malachy's, the Specials would puncture it with a bayonet, before returning it.

1942 Celtic cross inscription on B Wing wall.
Photo June 2008. [Author]

Life settled down for the Internees on C and D Wings and for the sentenced prisoners on A.Wing. Most outdoor sports organized by the Internees was on a piece of ground at the rear of D.Wing measuring about 60 feet by 60 feet; Gaelic and other classes continued, as did musical events. Arguments persisted over food, particularly breakfast and overcrowding continued with movement between C and D Wings.

The overcrowding became so bad, that the following October, 1942, 300 Internees were again transferred to Derry Gaol.

On the 6th February 1942, Thomas Walker, a warder, was shot by the IRA as he cycled along Durham Street. He was rushed to the RVH, but died within the hour.

Walker was well known among the Internees and his shooting came as a surprise, but it materialised he was shot in mistake for another named [*Withheld by author*], who it appears was the intended target.

An Easter commemoration parade of 1942 took place in the Gaol on Sunday 5th April

The Internees formed up in military formation in the yard after dinner and formed a square. The O.C read the 1916 proclamation, followed by a two minute silence.

They then paraded around the yard before being dismissed.

That evening, a *Ceilidh* was held, during which an oration was read by Neil Gillespie of Derry who had been the O.C on the *Al Rawdah*.

It was not unusual for clubs to be formed in the Gaol, as in May when Internees from Ballymacarrett formed the *Clann de Duide Gaelic Athletic and Social Club*.

Later in the year, the Sean Gaffney club was formed in Derry Gaol.

The following day, six young men were brought into the Gaol and housed on A.Wing following the shooting of an RUC member, Constable Patrick Murphy in the Clonard area.

Thus began one of the most emotive episodes of the forties periods within the Gaol.

The story of Tom Williams and his five co-accused has been well documented over the years; from his hanging on the 2nd September, 1942, to the long campaign to have his remains removed from the Gaol, which took place on Saturday 28th August 1999.

He was properly buried on Wednesday 19th January, 2000 from a packed St.Pauls church on the Falls Road.

This was followed by a huge commemoration on the Sunday, 23rd January from Clonard to Milltown Cemetery.

Alfie Hannaway was in the Fianna with Tom Williams. At sixteen, in 1940, young Alfie found himself interned in Derry Gaol after being arrested for drilling at the top of the Whiterock Road. At that time, he was the youngest Internee *to date*.

He recalled *"going down"* into the cells, as if underground, feeling a sense of isolation. Standing in the cell he heard voices and *"Belfast accents"*.

He pulled a table over to stand on it in an endeavour to reach a window. No sooner had he pulled himself on to the table in a bid if he could see anyone, when he was pulled to the ground by two warders who aggressively warned him not to attempt it again. It was purely a case of intimidation against a young man.

A scraped-out harp on B Wing wall, Photo June 2008. [Author]

From Derry, Alfie would be transferred to the *Al Rawdah* and then to Crumlin Road Gaol.

On the day set for Tom Williams's execution, the Gaol remained in a very sombre mood and an unusual air of silence took hold throughout the prison.

Billy Wiggins from the Marrowbone was one of those serving mass that morning and he recalled the emotional upset that had engulfed everyone.

Some prisoners were able to catch a glimpse of the box carrying his remains being carried toward the burial plot in the Gaol.

Billy Murray recalled:

> "I happened to step up on my stool to look over D.Wing yard and I also had a view of part of C.Wing, wood yard. I was just in time to see the end of the coffin carried by two warders going out of sight, up the wood yard toward the prison hospital and grave."

The other five men received life imprisonment having been reprieved, but they were released in October 1949.

There was an increase in IRA activity following Tom Williams's execution, although four weapons dumps found in and around farms at Hannastown on the outskirts of West Belfast, was to blunt planned actions in Belfast.

The haul yielded four Lewis machineguns, nine Thompson sub machine guns and seven rifles.

The sporadic IRA attacks had little impact, but two major escapes from both Crumlin Road and Derry Gaol in 1943, was a great moral boost to the Republican Movement, particularly as a tunnel out of D.Wing's Dining hall had been uncovered in the summer of 1942.

Jimmy Steele, Ned Maguire and Pat Donnelly made a daring escape from A.Wing on 15th January and then in March, a successful breakout was organized from Derry, only for the majority of the men to reinterned by the southern authorities.

Some did manage to stay active such as Seamus Burns [shot and killed on the 12th February, 1944], Harry O'Rawe, Albert Price, Paddy Meehan and Liam Perry.

By July 1943, there were 200 republican sentenced prisoners on A.Wing and both Jimmy Steele and Liam Burke were back in the Gaol following their re-capture.

Both men had been involved in the planning and execution of the Derry escape.

They were among eleven republicans who had heavy sentences imposed on them on the 3rd August, 1943 by Lord Justice Edward Murphy, a member of the Unionist Party, Orange Order and the Black Preceptory and the judge who sentenced Tom Williams to be executed. [Edward Murphy died three years later in 1945]

His Father was Attorney General James Murphy QC who was one of the Prosecuting Council against members of The Irish Nationalist Invincibles – [Fenian activists] who killed the Permanent under Secretary at the Irish office, Thomas Burke and the newly appointed Chief Secretary, Lord Frederick Cavendish, in Phoenix Park, Dublin on 6th May, 1882.

His role in the successful outcome earned him an appointment to the High Court. The family lived at Glencairn House, Leopardstown, County Dublin, later to become the official residence of the British Ambassador to Ireland.

Liam Burke simply remarked:

> *"I have nothing to say, as I do not recognise the right of Lord Justice Murphy to judge me."*

Jimmy Steele commented: *"I have nothing to say to this British Assembly".*

While Alfie White said: *"I do not plead with my enemy"*

Jimmy Steele, Liam Burke and Hugh Mc Ateer were released in August 1950, the last of the *"Forties men"* to leave Crumlin Road Gaol.

The 1943 escape created a vindictive surge of ill-treatment by some warders against men held on A.Wing, which continued through-out that year. The standard of food was poor and the cleanliness of eating utensils was at times disgusting.

The IRA continued to remain intact, but in reality it was simply carrying the mantle and holding together a framework of a republican tradition that still believed in physical force action.

At the beginning of May 1945, WW11 came to an end with the unconditional surrender of German forces. By July, word spread around the Gaol that the Internees were to be released and by the end of the month they began to walk out the gates of Crumlin Road Gaol.

"My most vivid memory of the jail was being taken through the tunnel into the courthouse for the first time - it was an eerie experience!"

James Quinn, former nationalist prisoner, 1971

"You were unlocked in the mornings, you got out for breakfast - if you wanted; I don't think I got up for breakfast in the whole seven months - not for a bowl of cornflakes and a bit of sausage or potato bread floating about in gallons of grease.

David Ervine, former loyalist prisoner and P.U.P. leader

"I was back in the Crum in 1982, the cockroaches plagued us in the cell, they were walking up the walls and you had to pull your bed away from the wall as they were everywhere.

Malachy Murray, former republican prisoner.

"On my second tour, in 1972, we were deployed to Gridwood barracks in the New Lodge. During this time we were briefed that prisoners in the Crumlin road Gaol had rioted and taken prison officers prisoner, and that we were to get them out, which we did after a bit of a battle.

Former marine, from the book 'A Long Long War' by Ken Wharton

CHAPTER 4:
ARMED CONFLICT TO PEACE - 1969 - 2007.

Following the end of WW11, Republican Internees walked free from Crumlin Road Gaol in July 1945. For some, it had been over six years of incarceration which included the Gaol, the *SS Al Rawdah* and Derry Prison. Men returned home in poor health, their lives left in a dysfunctional state and now having to begin to re-build relationships and family life.

For men like Billy Murray, it was the second time their lives had been forcefully disrupted by Internment without trail. Throughout the country, north and south, republicans were released to find a movement fragmented by politics and policy of direction.

But the IRA, as in the twenties, always manages to rise against adversity and re-build its structure, setting a course to focus on, primarily the north. Now under the command of Tony Magan, a series of raids were authorised against British Barracks, mainly in the north.

The most successful of these was carried out on Saturday, 12th June 1954, when a daring raid on *Gough* Barracks in Armagh, netted 340 rifles, 37 Sten Sub-machineguns, twelve Bren guns and forty training rifles. The Barracks was home to the Royal Irish Fusiliers and the raid was carried out by volunteers of the Dublin IRA.

Security at the Barracks was poor and this greatly aided the sixteen IRA, who had not only infiltrated the base, but had planned it to precession. Another raid in October against *St.Lucia* Barracks in Omagh ended in a gun-battle and the capture of eight of the IRA unit. Five soldiers were wounded along with two IRA volunteers.

The captured men were tried and sentenced to 10-12 years penal servitude in Crumlin Road Gaol. Eamonn Boyce, from Dublin, 12 years ; Tom Mitchell, Dublin, 10 years ; Paddy Kearney, Dublin, 10 years; Liam Mulcahy, Cork, 10 years; John Mc Cabe, Dublin, 10 years;

Sean Hegarty, Cork, 10 years; Sean O'Callaghan, Cork, 10 years; Philip Clarke, Dublin, 10 years.

OMAGH PRISONERS

EAMONN BOYCE (Dublin) Sentenced to 12 years penal servitude.

TOM MITCHELL (Dublin) Sentenced to 10 years penal servitude.

PADDY KEARNEY (Dublin) Sentenced to 10 years penal servitude.

LIAM MULCAHY (Cork) 10 years penal servitude.
JOHN McCABE (Dublin) 10 years penal servitude.
SEAN HEGARTY (Cork) 10 years penal servitude.
SEAN O'CALLAGHAN (Cork) 10 years penal servitude.
PHILIP CLARKE (Dublin) 10 years penal servitude.

St.Lucia Barracks was the Home Depot of the Inniskilling Fusiliers.

The fact that the IRA were in action again, was enough to maintain morale and attract new volunteers for a Northern Campaign.

The Republican Movement was further encouraged by the Westminster elections that year, when two of those imprisoned for their part in the Omagh raid, Thomas Mitchell and Phillip Clarke, were elected on an abstentionist policy of non-recognition of the British Parliament.

Phillip Clarke was elected for Fermanagh/South Tyrone - [The same seat Bobby Sands would win during the 1981 Hunger Strike] and Tom Mitchell was elected for Mid-Ulster - [A seat in more recent times won and held by Sinn Fein].

Tomas Mac Curtain and Manus Canning polled very high in Armagh and Derry, while Patrick Kearney stood in the strong Unionist seat of South Belfast.

Under the Unionist controlled northern administration, their mandate was not recognised as they were imprisoned in Crumlin Road Gaol.

Tom Mitchell having been disqualified despite his win in Mid-Ulster, embarrassed the Unionist regime when he won the seat for a second time during a by-election held on the 11th August, 1955. Mitchell increased his majority vote, but this was deemed ineligible and once again he was disqualified for being a prisoner in Crumlin Road Gaol and the seat went to a Unionist. [He was released from *Crumlin Road* in July, 1961]

The IRA *Border Campaign* as it became known was planned to direct attacks against the RUC and B Specials in the hope of drawing in the British Army and thus create an atmosphere of British repression, which, it was hoped, would trigger off a massive popular reaction on both sides of the border.

This was to be achieved by means of twelve Flying Columns, which would simultaneously carry out attacks on Customs and RUC posts along the border. This was to be followed up by attacks on RUC Barracks.

The campaign opened up on the night of 11th December, 1956, as rain, sleet and snow lashed down the length of the border.

Fortunes were mixed for the IRA that *weather beaten* night, but two days later they had more success against the RUC Barracks in Lisnaskea and later at Derrylin and Rosslea, in Fermanagh. [In the recent conflict, these locations had to be heavily fortified by the British Army due to sustained IRA attacks, the aim that proved beyond the grasp of the 1957 volunteers]

In reality, the logistics to sustain these attacks were simply not there. Many Nationalist people although sympathetic to their cause, were not supportive of an all-out campaign of conflict.

A major drawback was that the volunteers were unfamiliar with the geography of the area, being from the south, and there was also a hostile Unionist population in these areas to contend with.

Their opponents in the RUC and Specials had a comprehensive knowledge of the social geography of their areas, which enabled them to shut down any sympathetic safe houses.

The IRA was at times forced to operate out of dark and freezing tunnel-hides cut into inhospitable hillsides. A makeshift first-aid post was established underground on the Monaghan border.

The worst aspect that led to the failure of this short campaign was that De Valera once more introduced Internment in line with the north, which closed down any safe ground and led to the arrest of republicans across the south.

Belfast republicans despite playing no major role in the events taking place along the border counties were also arrested and Interned in *Crumlin Road*.

Just as during the war years, when some men who had been firstly interned in 1922/1923, were re-interned, some of those wartime internees found themselves re-incarcerated again for no reason other than that they were republicans.

Attempts at escape and the digging of a tunnel became a natural course to follow for men who were beginning to feel that they knew the *"Crum"*, as well as they knew their own home environment.

However, what they or the Unionist Parliament at Stormont did not know then, was that this would be the third and final time that the instrument of Internment would prove to be the prime weapon in the armoury of the northern regime.

The next time they would resort to their *ace card* of repression, the result would be catastrophic.

The "Border Campaign" had ranged from roads being cratered, to attacks on Custom Posts and RUC Barracks, but by 26th February 1962, it was over, with a *"Dump Arms"* order.

The Republican Movement began to reassess itself and it was generally agreed that the movement needed to develop a coherent political philosophy that had some relevance to modern day thinking, but the idea of moving toward a left-wing, or Marxist style philosophy, was a step in the wrong direction, particularly for the traditionalists.

It may have fitted in well to the trend of the sixties, but it took little account of the historical realities of the north and this was to prove the crucial principle that was to paralyse the mainstream movement when sectarian violence broke out in October, 1968.

When republicans were released from Crumlin Road Gaol in 1961, the IRA in Belfast was at an all-time low. It had been in a serious state by the late fifties. Billy Mc Kee, the Belfast O.C stated that the weapons situation was so grave, that when the Quartermaster came over to Leeson Street from Ballymacarrett, he was able to move a *"weapons dump"* in a suitcase. *

*[Conversation with Historian Sean O'Coinn, 1998]

Upon his release from *Crumlin Road*, Billy Mc Kee began to re-build the IRA in Belfast. Men such as Sean Mc Nally, whose Father, Jack had been interned during the war years, *reported back* the day he was released from *Crumlin Road* in 1961.

He happened to meet Bridget Hannan, a prominent figure in Cumann Na mBan, who advised him to *"Speak to Billy Mc Kee"* *[Sean Mc Nally to Sean O'Coinn]

Stalwarts, such as Jimmy Steele, Liam Burke, Gerry Maguire, and Jimmy Drumm would be there in the re-build, alongside men such as Proinsias Mac Airt, Leo Martin, Sean Mc Nally, Billy O'Neill and Tom O'Donnell.

Unfortunately, the leadership in Dublin grew steadily more remote from the rank and file in most of the country.

Under the control of Dublin man Cathal Goulding, now Chief of Staff, communications became tenuous, as the leadership sat in the capitol planning their policy of social and economic agitation.

The movement's energies were now poured into poor housing conditions and the rights of the fishermen. This is good sound politics in a stable and democratic society, but it was not going to defend Nationalist districts in Belfast, should sectarian violence erupt again

"The day of the Thompson is over", Goulding told Mc Kee*

*[Conversation with Sean O' Coinn, 1998]

This was going to create tensions between republicans in the north and the leadership in Dublin and in 1963, Billy Mc Kee resigned, being replaced by a Goulding supporter, Billy Mc Millan.

The sixties were a "Decade of Change", the world was rapidly changing as a new generation took to the streets, demanding civil rights and equality, particularly in the United States.

Disillusionment with the Vietnam War began to over-spill as television images brought the scenes of war into the American "Living Room". In Paris and London, CND and anti-war rallies turned into clashes with the police as another generation took *its* viewpoint and belief for a "fair and better world" on to the streets.

In the tiny state that was Northern Ireland, the drive for civil rights came very much to the fore in 1968. The sixties began to show signs that blatant economic discrimination against the Nationalists in the north was *softening, but still embedded in the fibre of Unionist society.*

A reasonably-sized Catholic middle class had started to form, the result, to a large extent, of the British 1948 Education Act which established a grants system and opened up higher education to the working class. By the mid-sixties, the children of Catholic publicans and Bookmakers, who could be funded by their parents, went to university.

It was the Bar trade, Driving jobs, and the Docks, that provided work among Catholic working-class men, as the engineering factories and shipbuilding skilled apprenticeships, were in the main, kept within Unionism.

A wrong name, school, or address, could in itself be enough to be turned down for a job.

The Prime Minister at Stormont was Terence O'Neill, a man who fostered Liberalism, but who led a Unionist party that could not tolerate change and he therefore reduced himself to trying to improve relations between north and south, and in the north itself, between the two communities.

However, his inability to translate his desires into actual and concrete reform increased Catholic frustration. The problem with the O'Neill led government was that although it promoted Liberalism that raised Catholic expectations, it dodged real reform.

A climate of dissatisfaction was created and powerful currents began to run through the community, resulting in the emergence of the Northern Ireland Civil Rights Association.

Their campaign was to obtain civil rights in housing, jobs and to demand a single non-transferable vote and the redrawing of electoral boundaries.

It also called for the repeal of the Special Powers Act and the disbandment of the B.Specials.

There was no mention of armed struggle, or a United Ireland, or a war against the British. It was purely to fight for equality in housing and employment and the basic right of fair practice, without religious discrimination.

This drive for civil rights caused an insecure Stormont Government to over-react to such an extent with police violence that an over-spill of resentment and frustration at decades of discrimination, resulted in serious rioting on a scale never before experienced.

Shocking scenes of how the RUC reacted to the protesting marchers prompted the Labour government in London to order the Stormont parliament to institute reforms without delay.

Terence O'Neill responded with a willingness to implement reforms in housing and to address other grievances.

Suddenly, not only the British media, but the international media began to focus on this small corner of Ireland and the ferocity of televised street violence which was sweeping this little known part of the United Kingdom.

Terence O'Neill was genuine in his efforts to create change. He dismissed his Minister for Home Affairs, William Craig, [who opposed reform], from the cabinet, but events were about to overtake him, as the north was spiralling toward all out conflict in the Nationalist working-class areas of Belfast and Derry.

As O'Neill was attempting to stabilise the state, Cathal Goulding was facing calls to act in protecting Civil Rights marchers from the RUC and B.Specials. Goulding knew he had to do something, but was also reluctant to get drawn into armed action in the north.

But just as events would overtake Terence O'Neill, Republicanism now also found itself at a crossroads of political advancement to the Left, or traditional armed action in defence of the Nationalists in the north. The cast was set.

In April 1969, Terence O'Neill was forced to resign as the *hawks* in his cabinet refused to support his reforms. His most bitter opponent was Brian Faulkner and his position was filled by his cousin, James Chichester Clark. The day that O'Neill was forced to resign, 19th April, 1969, could be defined as probably the first major crack in the fall of the Stormont regime.

That same day, serious rioting had broken out in the *Bogside* area of Derry, with large sections of the RUC turning into a sectarian mob attacking people, even in their homes.

This was to become *the torch that lit the flame*, as a Defence Committee, made up of a wide representation of the community, was established in preparation for any similar violent incursions.

When the expected trouble came on Tuesday 12th August 1969, it climaxed into a two-day running battle between the Bogside community and the RUC.

As the RUC pushed back the Nationalist crowds from William Street into the Bogside, the Nationalists fell back on to prepared barricades, and then as the RUC advanced into the narrow streets around the Bogside in armoured vehicles and on foot, they were brought to a standstill by a sustained barrage of bricks, bottles and petrol bombs.

Across the east flank of Little James Street, the RUC encountered barricades, as they battled up toward the main Rossville Street area, were the high-rise flats provided ideal height to launch down petrol bombs on the RUC lines.

The running battle highlighted a community in revolt as the Irish flag flew from the top of the flats, a symbol of the Nationalist community regaining their area.

Radio *Free Derry* broadcast from a radio transmitter sat up in the Creggan estate and appealed for help, particularly to the southern government.

Television pictures went around the world, as an exhausted RUC lolled in the narrow streets, demoralised and fatigued. They had failed after two days of serious rioting to penetrate the Bogside barricades and re-in-store order. Their commander requested the B.Specials be brought in, who were already waiting on stand-by with their Lee Enfield rifles and Sten sub-machine guns.

Had the Specials been deployed and the blood-letting really commenced, Free State troops would have had to cross the Donegal border, prepared, or not, and match the empty rhetoric coming from the Fianna Fail Taoiseach, Jack Lynch in Dublin, of *"Not standing idly by"*

As it was, British troops, not Free State troops, arrived in the centre of Derry, at *teatime* on the afternoon of Thursday, 14th August 1969, when soldiers of the 1st Battalion, Prince of Wales Own', deployed into Waterloo Place and fanned out into the Bogside, much to the dismay of republicans, such as Sean Keenan who had played a key role in the defence, despite having little weapons.

The British Army ware now back on the streets of Derry for the first time since the 1920-22 periods.

In Belfast, the situation grew tense as the Unionist/Protestant community believed the events in Derry that they were witnessing on their TV screens, was the beginning of a Republican insurrection. This was not helped by the RUC who backed the insurrection plot, and deployed Shoreland Armoured cars mounted with Browning 0.30-inch medium machine-guns, into Hasting Street Barracks at the foot of the Falls Road.

In reality, any notion of an IRA rising in Belfast during August 1969 was no more than an obsession of fear by the Unionist Parliament. They only had around active 80 volunteers in the city and arms dumps had been depleted, some of which had been moved south.

This obsession had begun three years earlier in 1966, as republicans commemorated the 50th anniversary of the 1916 rising throughout Ireland, including Belfast.

Elements within Unionism began to manipulate fear and suspicion among the Protestant working-class, as they did in the thirties, from which emerged two groups; Ulster Protestant Volunteers and the Ulster Volunteer Force-[UVF].

This coincided with the rise of Rev.Ian Paisley's firebrand style of politics.

The small UVF group was based in the Shankill area of Belfast, numbering around twelve men.

These two groups engaged in a number of attacks in May and June of 1966 which included throwing petrol bombs at Holy Cross Catholic Girls school, to the unintentional killing of a Protestant pensioner in her home [Matilda Gould], when a Catholic owned public house on Upper Charleville Street off the Shankill Road was petrol bombed, to the murder of two innocent Catholic men, simply killed because of their religion.

As a result of the murders, five men were arrested, and in October, Gusty Spence, the alleged leader of the group was sentenced to life imprisonment, to serve a minimum of twenty years in Crumlin Road Gaol, although he always denied that he was directly involved in the murders of the two Catholic men, and in particular, Peter Ward.

Thus, the first Loyalist prisoners entered the Gaol: Gusty Spence, Hugh McClean, and Robert Williamson.

At the end of June 1966, Terence O'Neill proscribed the UVF as an illegal organisation, stating on the 29th June that:

> *"Let no one imagine that there is any connection what-so-ever between men who were ready to die for the country on the fields of France and a sordid conspiracy of criminals prepared to take up arms against unprotected citizens."*

He even had Ian Paisley arrested in July and imprisoned in *Crumlin Road* for a few months for a breach of the peace. This led to a large crowd demonstrating outside the Gaol, where the Reverend was confined in a cell at the bottom of B.2.

As the Bogside community was battling against the RUC in Derry, rioting broke out on Divis Street in Belfast on Wednesday, 13th August, between crowds of Nationalist youths and the RUC.

At one point, an RUC Humber armoured car came under gun attack at Leeson Street and a grenade was thrown. This convinced the RUC that the IRA was taking a lead in the escalating rioting and as a result, Shoreland Armoured cars were deployed from Hasting Street Barracks and deployed into the narrow tightly bound Divis area .

A large crowd of young men from Divis began erecting barricades and surged toward Hasting Street Barrack confronting the RUC with petrol bombs.

The following day, Stormont mobilized the B.Specials and the news was flashed that afternoon. To the Nationalist/Catholic community, this armed Protestant militia amounted to only one thing; aggressive conflict.

That afternoon, a running battle commenced along Divis Street as the RUC Armoured cars advanced toward the Divis Flats complex, sending crowds running in different directions, including into Dover and Percy Street that led toward the Unionist Shankill Road District.

At the top end of these streets, several hundred Protestants had gathered behind a line of armed B.Specials and they began to surge down the interlinking streets between the Falls and Shankill Road, attacking Catholic homes in the *mixed* streets.

Nationalists now found themselves having to battle the RUC, while pushing back the Protestant crowds and B.Specials to prevent them from entering Divis Street.

As in Derry, the Nationalists used the Divis Flats complex and the roofs of the flats to their advantage, launching petrol bomb attacks against the RUC.

The rioting stretched the length of Divis Street amid the intersecting streets that led toward the Shankill Road. Catholic homes mid-way down Conway Street and Northumberland Street were now ablaze, as the Nationalist stronghold left of Divis Street, the *Pound Loney*, was barricaded and crowds surged out into Divis Street with petrol bombs to defend the area.

As the RUC launched baton charges against the Nationalist crowds, a man emerged from the melee, dropped on one knee and opened fire with a pistol. Then at midnight, crowds from the Shankill reached the Dover Street/Divis Street junction, only to be fired on from Gilford Street by an IRA volunteer, using a .38 revolver. A Protestant man was killed, which forced a response by the RUC, which was either, panic, or a total intent at murder!

Their Shoreland Armoured cars began sweeping tracer bullets with .30 calibre Browning machine-guns along Divis Street toward the flats complex, indiscriminately hitting thirteen of the flats with gunfire. RUC men positioned on top of the Barracks were also firing down into the street.

The crews of these armoured cars had insufficient training in the use of the Browning's and should not have been deployed into a built up area, such as Divis Street.

Four high velocity bullets pierced two walls of one low level flat before entering the room of nine-year-old Patrick Rooney, killing the child as he sheltered with his brothers and sister in the bedroom. Another fatality was Trooper Mc Cabe, home on leave from his regiment, the Queens Royal Irish Hussars. He was hit, while trying to help another man on one of the balcony's, and died instantly.

It is most probable that Trooper Mc Cabe was shot by an RUC member firing from the roof of Hasting Street Barrack.

With a lull in the shooting, Catholic families in Dover Street, Percy Street and Beverley Street, struggled to recover whatever possessions they could, and made their way to shelter across Divis Street, reminiscent of 1920.

The Broadway Cinema was *opened up* by the IRA and used as a temporary shelter for people fleeing their homes that night.

As the early hours of Friday morning ticked past midnight, another crowd of around 200 carrying petrol bombs surged down Dover Street from the Shankill end of the street attempting again to break out into Divis Street. The warm dark night was illuminated with the red flames that splattered from the burning terrace houses, now evacuated by their Catholic owners. The smell of burning, crackling ashes drifted into the smoke-filled air that seemed to blanket the night sky.

The crowd was met by opposing Nationalists, using anything they could muster to prevent any further burning of homes in Divis Street by the mobs.

By 2am, the situation appeared to becoming critical, as gunfire and petrol bombs ware now being directed into Divis Street around St, Comgall's school and the Maisonettes facing Percy Street. The school sat in a commanding position and earlier in the evening, the IRA had positioned men into the school, but these were later withdrawn.[The IRA could only operate in small units of three to six men, as only around thirty were active that night.]

But desperation quickly turned to one of confidence, as a group of armed men moved into the back of the school; former IRA volunteers, who had been despondent over the Goulding policy of disarming. This small group had mustered a few weapons and were now a thin line of defence to prevent a critical situation, becoming even worst.

Taking up positions, Billy Mc Kee, Albert Price, Seamus Twomey, and Liam Burke, began directing fire across toward Percy Street, scattering the crowds down the street. * [*A Rebel Voice*, Quinn R.J. 1998]

Gunfire was returned by the Specials, and bullets showered the wall and ground in front of the school from a firing position on top of Andrew's Mill * *[Billy Mc Kee, to Sean O'Coinn, 1998]

For an hour and half, the defenders kept up a stream of gunfire, only leaving when their ammunition was spent. Eight Protestants were shot and wounded and this small, but crucial action, prevented even greater destruction.

On the morning of Friday, 15th August, 1969, General Freeland only had at his disposal, three Companies of the newly arrived 1st Battalion, Royal Regiment of Wales, and two Companies of the Garrison Battalion, 2nd Queen's Regiment, to cover Belfast.

Reinforcements were being mustered to be flown in on Saturday morning, but when the RUC Commissioner reported to the Stormont Minister of Home Affairs, Robert Porter, that the RUC could not cope with a further night's rioting, troops were requested from London.

In London, the British Home Secretary, James Callaghan, faced a press briefing.

With the newspapers full of stories and pictures of the burning of Belfast and facing challenging questions from reporters, James Callaghan, pre-empted Stormont and reassured the press: *"Gentlemen"*, he announced, *"the troops are going into Belfast"*.

Belfast, August 1969

British Army checkpoint, Durham Street

Falls Road / Albert Street, August 1969

BURNED OUT HOUSES Bombay street, Clonard, August 1969

Burned out houses in Bombay Street, August 1969

A few hours later, around 3pm, soldiers began to deploy from Durham Street, into Divis Street and up toward Conway Street.

However, their presence failed to prevent the burning of Bombay Street and attacks on Catholic homes in Cupar Street, in the Clonard area, north-west of Divis Street. The military, did not understand the sectarian geography of Belfast, or the environment they had suddenly been thrust into.

To the north and east, the Clonard is bordered by the semi-circle of Cupar Street, to the south, by the Falls Road, and to the west, by the Springfield Road. As in 1920, Catholic homes came under attack in Cupar Street, with families having to flee into the inner Clonard, were again, Billy Mc Kee and a handful of IRA veterans, did their best to protect homes and the monastery with a handful of pistols, and a couple of .22 rifles.

NEWSPAPER 1969

A young teenager, Gerard Mc Auley, aged fifteen, a member of *Na Fianna Eireann,* was shot by a sniper as he was helping families evacuate possessions from their homes in Bombay Street, which had born the brunt of the attack on the Clonard.

That evening, a reinforcement Battalion, the 3rd Light Infantry landed at RAF Aldergrove and drove straight to north Belfast, deploying along the Crumlin Road, amid the Catholic Ardoyne, which had also been attacked, resulting in the death of two innocent men, of one whom was shot by the RUC with an SMG- 9mm Sterling Sub machinegun as he stood in his home in Herbert Street.

The main trouble centred on Hooker Street, Herbert Street, and Butler Street, as the RUC used Humber Armoured cars to force their way in through barricades erected by Nationalists. The RUC were firing Sterling submachine guns, claiming they had been fired at, but their fire was indiscriminate in nature, and they made no effort to prevent Protestant crowds from launching petrol bombs into the Nationalist streets.

Between July and August, 1969, ten people were killed and 900 were injured. Two hundred homes were burned and double that number damaged, with 1,820 families driven from their homes; 1,505 were Catholic, and 315 were Protestant, every one, no matter their religion, a shameful and tragic occurrence.

Thus, were the opening events of what is often termed as *"The Troubles".*

The deployment of those first troops, which by September 1969, had reached 6,000, was to mark a British deployment that, unknown then during those initial weeks of turmoil, would last until 2007; the peak being reached in 1972, with 21,000 troops.

The cost in lives to Britain amounted to, 1,441 British military personnel; 722 of whom were killed in paramilitary attacks and 719 of who died as a result of other causes.

British soldier on the Falls Road. 14th August 1969

That figure consisted **of all military personnel**; broken down, 814 were from the regular Army, 477 of whom were killed, and 337 who died as a result of other causes.

In total, the conflict overall was to cause 3,722 lives, between the years 1966-2007.

Following the events of August 1969, the political situation began to rapidly change. In October, Britain moved and forced Stormont to disband the B.Specials, which led to rioting on the Shankill Road between Loyalists and the British Army, resulting in the death of the first RUC member of the conflict, killed by a *Loyalist* gunman.

British troops also "opened fire" for the first time since their deployment.

The Republican Movement faced fundamental internal change as a result of what had happened in Belfast and Derry during August, and this led to the creation of a new Provisional IRA who moved away from the Goulding left-wing leadership. This new movement fell under the leadership of those veterans who had been disaffected by Goulding's policies following the failed "Border Campaign". They began to re-equip and re-arm, recruiting among a new, younger generation of Nationalists, egger to *"hit back"* at the Unionist state.

By 1970, signs of a break down in relations between the Nationalist community and the British Army began to appear; not with any big impact, *but the cracks were beginning to show*. In March of that year, serious rioting broke out in the Nationalist areas of Ballymurphy and Upper Springfield in Belfast, which saw soldiers of the 1st Battalion, Royal Scots aggressively move in and indiscriminately cover the streets with CS gas canisters, engulfing homes in the process.

The following month, on the 9th May, twenty-seven soldiers were injured during rioting in the New Lodge district of North Belfast.

However, if one event is to be recorded as the most definite landmark that launched the north into open conflict for the next 30 years and marked the Provisional IRA as a group destined to become a major Guerrilla Force and one of the most effective in the world, it is *"The Battle of St.Matthew's"*, and the events that occurred around the Springfield, Ardoyne and Ballymacarrett/Short Strand districts over the weekend period of 27th/28th June, 1970.

The months of June and July, are traditionally what are referred to in the north, as *"the marching season"*, when the Loyal Orange Lodges engage in various parades of commemoration, culminating on the 12th July, celebrating a battle deemed significant to the Protestant faith in the north, dating back to 1690.

Troops in the Falls District Belfast July 1970

The morning of Saturday the 27th June, 1970, burst open over Belfast's Crumlin Road with the sun playing on the slate roofs of the neatly compact rows of terraces, as smoke from the morning fires went curling into the still air; the housewife's sweeping the debris of another night of rioting away from doorways that were protected with an almost obsessive sense of pride.

Looking on, bewildered and grey faced, tired British soldiers paced up and down, or just sat in their land rovers, perched behind scratched Perspex shields trying to steal ten minutes sleep, but still aware of the hostile environment that Belfast had now in places, become to them. The months of April and May had seen a steady increase in rioting and sporadic shooting incidents between Nationalist and Unionist districts.

It cast a scene as normal as could be for a city steadily growing under military occupation for those working-class districts, long steeped in the history of Belfast's sectarian strife.

In the Protestant streets off the Crumlin Road and in the distant direction of the Shankill, the tremulous wail of bagpipes, flutes and Lambeg drums could be heard, tuning and scaling for the day ahead. As the Orange Brethren gathered across Belfast, the British Army's calendar in their Thiepval Barracks HQ in Lisburn, ten miles south of Belfast, marked the day *"As a possibly tricky time"*. This *"tricky time"*, as one junior Intelligence officer had marked it, was to develop into the most definitive landmark event of the recent conflict, one for which the British government must take responsibility, if not the blame, for a costly mistake that one senior civil servant, Ronald Borroughs referred to as:

> *"the greatest single miscalculation, I have ever saw in the course of my whole life"*.

The Orangemen and their accompanying bands had begun to assemble in Loyalist/Unionist districts around lunch-time, on what was a warm, bright June day.

This was the *"mini-twelfth"*, when the Orange parades reach fever pitch in the run up to the main 12th July parades. Old, and middle-aged men, proudly donning their lodge sashes, assembled in serried ranks behind the senior brethren who carried polished swords, while young teenagers threw staves twirling into the air, dancing in turn to the flute.

Once again, they would rally to the sound of the Lambeg drums, march to the flute and revel in sectarian party tunes, marching pass the streets of their Catholic neighbours flaunting provocative anti-Catholic symbols.

There was without doubt, a grave narrow-minded sectarian attitude that was academic of all that was wrong about the Unionist-controlled state, yet among this cavalcade of *Orangeism,* there was, it has to be said, many liberal minded people, who genuinely wished to simply express their faith and beliefs without being offensive to their Catholic neighbours. But they were lost amid the bigotry that these parades appeared to represent.

But on this day, triumphalism, was about to turn sour and the first major crack in the northern state was about to open. Despite frantic efforts by the Nationalist Citizens Defence Central Committee to have the parades re-routed away from passing sensitive Nationalist areas, Stormont refused to recognise the volatile situation and refused.

The parade was to be led this year by No.9 District, who began to leave New Barnsley at around 1.30pm to proceed out on to the Upper Springfield Road to march and join the main parade. A band leading this small feeder parade began its march with the Orange anthem, *"The sash, my Father wore."*

Soldiers were positioned to contain a small crowd of Nationalists who had gathered, an exchange of abuse took place between the youths and the parade.

Then within minutes, several hundred Nationalist youths appeared from the Whiterock Road and launched into the parade, sending it scattering down the Springfield Road.

A running battle now ensued as hundreds of troops flooded into the area amid burning barricades; serious rioting ensued that would last into the evening, cumulating in Protestant families fleeing their homes in New Barnsley, some wrecking them before departure.

It would be the final time an Orange parade would leave New Barnsley as the reality of segregated areas began to take shape, and would reach frightening proportion by August 1971.

The rioting at Upper Springfield was only the beginning, as tension began to accumulate in the Nationalist enclaves of Clonard, Ardoyne, Unity Flats - [Carrickhill] and the Ballymacarrett / Short Strand districts.

The newly formed Companies of the Provisional IRA were put on stand-by in the respective districts, and in the Short Strand a well-armed local Citizens Defence Group stood ready to support the local IRA Company, which was comprised mainly of young men with basic training, but armed and prepared to engage and counter any potential attack on their district.

As the day progressed, the IRA opened fire close to the Clonard and in a more serious incident; gunfire broke out close to Ardoyne on the Crumlin Road, when the IRA again opened fire at a hostile crowd. For over a thirty-minute period the shooting continued, and as a result of both incidents, three Protestant civilians had been killed.

It was apparent, there was going to be no repeat, of August 1969.

But it was to the east of the city, where *the spark would be lit.*

That evening, news was spreading through Unionist districts of the shooting and of Protestant homes being evacuated at New Barnsley. In the Unionist heartland of East Belfast, crowds began to gather on the Newtownards Road, as trouble broke out close to the Nationalist Seaforde Street area, and St.Matthew's Catholic Church, which was on the edge of the Nationalist area of Ballymacarrett/Short Strand.

The same conflict points, the same streets, the same houses, that had witnessed the vicious fighting of 1921, were again to the fore as history began to repeat itself amid the petrol bombs and gunfire that now took hold around the Short Strand.

As in 1920, any Catholic owned Public House outside of the Nationalist area, was burned and looted by the mobs, as petrol bombs were launched toward St.Matthew's church.

But as the light faded and the glow of the flames lit into the sky, the peel of rifle and machine-gun fire shattered the mobs as the IRA and Citizen Defence volunteers opened fire.

The crowds scattered, many wounded, as the fire swept along the area around the church. Barricades had been erected at vantage points within the Short Strand and armed men positioned to repel any incursions, as a heavy gun-battle took hold around the Nationalist district.

The Army was stretched to the limit and could do little to intervene, instead conducting a containment policy, while the RUC contributed little in the way of protection.

What was apparent is, the Loyalists were left shocked at the extent of the gunfire coming down on them and any attempt to break into the Short Strand, was aggressively repelled.

The battle lasted until Dawn, when the Army finally managed to get into Ballymacarrett in sufficient numbers to take control of the area, but the damage was done and the cast was set for the Provisional IRA to emerge as the *defenders of the Nationalist people.*

For IRA leaders such as Billy Mc Kee, now the Provisional Belfast Brigade O.C, it run deeper than that; for him, it was a case, that this time, they had the ability to prevent another Bombay Street, another Percy Street, and another Conway Street!

There have been many stories and incorrect versions of what is now commonly referred to as the *"Battle of St.Matthew's"*. Loyalists believe the Short Strand had been flooded with IRA men from all over Belfast that night to deliberately attack them. Other versions talk of Billy Mc Kee and a handful of IRA men positioned in the grounds of the church firing machine-guns against the attacking mobs, and that was the extent of the battle.

The reality was none of those versions are historically correct, and the IRA in the Short Strand that night, were in the main, local volunteers, along with three Provisional Brigade officers from outside the area that included Billy Mc Kee, and two, possibly three, non-local volunteers.

The gun-battle itself increased in ferocity, with the defenders very much in control. After Billy Mc Kee had been wounded and taken out of the district, the area returned under the command of its own O.C, Thomas O' Donnell, [who died in May 1973]. The role of the local Citizens Defence Group was also paramount in the outcome, which resulted in upwards of forty being wounded, and two civilians killed. One Nationalist Defender was also killed, and Billy Mc Kee wounded in *accidental friendly fire.*

Within days of the Short Strand battle, angry Unionist politicians were calling for the Army to move against the IRA. Raids into the Short Strand followed, but it was the Falls Road the Army primarily targeted, and following serious rioting and a gun battle with both the Official and Provisional IRA, they imposed a curfew on the area, creating a more hostile environment between the Nationalists and the British Army; Stormont was guiding British Government policy in a direction that was spiralling toward all out conflict.

With the Provisional IRA now re-equipped with a large shipment of weapons, it planned to begin "offensive" action against the state. By 1971, whatever atmosphere of peaceful relations that had existed between the broad base of Nationalists and the British Army had eroded, as troops stepped up raids on Nationalist districts of Belfast.

In February 1971, following rioting, bomb attacks and sniping in Ardoyne and the New Lodge districts, the first British soldier, Gunner Robert Curtis, aged 20, of the 156 [*Inkerman*] Battery, 94 Locating Regiment, Royal Artillery, died on active service.

The following month, trouble broke out across all Nationalist districts, and on the 12th February, 1971, twelve bombs exploded as the IRA was engaging in a bombing campaign against commercial targets. By May 1971, 136 explosions had been recorded across the north, by the end of the year that would have reached a total of, 1,022.

Amid this increase of sustained IRA activity, Unionist politicians began calling for Internment. The new Stormont P.M Brian Faulkner was constantly lobbying Westminster to introduce Internment, which General Tuzo, the G.O.C of 39th Infantry Brigade in the north, referred to as the *"Unionist Panacea"*.

By July 1971, with the IRA now bombing Belfast, Derry and other towns on a daily basis, Internment was finally endorsed by the British Government. It was not the preferred choice, but at the same time, it knew stability and public confidence was under threat.

There were ninety-one bombings that month, and economic life was suffering.

General Tuzo may not have been enthusiastic about Internment, but when he received his orders to implement it, he would do so, *and go in hard.*

The days of a Head Constable and three policemen turning up at the door of a republican and arresting him for internment in *Crumlin Road* were over. If Internment was to be implemented, it would need British troops to enter these now hostile areas.

Beechfield Street, Short Strand late, on Internment day, 9th August 1971, after the British Army had gained a foothold. Note the Paras in the street.

The final decision came at a Cabinet meeting in Downing Street in London on Thursday the 5th August, with Faulkner in attendance to give his analysis of why in his experience, he felt it would work. But he was drawing on the success of the past and times had changed. *He was confident and rearing to go,* a confidence that would prove disastrous within the next few weeks.

General Tuzo flew back to his H.Q at Thiepval Barracks and began the logistics for *"Operation Demetrius"* set for Monday, 9th August.

When it came in the early hours of Monday, 3,000 troops moved against Nationalist districts across the north. In Belfast and Derry, it was met with a surge of resistance, never before saw in the history of the state.

Troops arrived at doors, some with blacken faces forcefully rapping up the occupants, others had their doors broken, as men, young and old were taken from their beds, some still in pyjamas covered with a quick coat grabbed from a hook.

Madrid Street Edgar Street looking toward Beechfield Street. Short Strand
August 1971 [Martin Meyer]

Women were verbally abused and the cry of children ignored as fathers and husbands were pushed into the back of a waiting Saracen armoured personnel carrier en route for an interrogation centre.

Women and girls formed up amid the terrace streets, banging dustbin lids, a crude, but effective signalling system which echoed across the small back-to-back houses with a high pitched shrill, while whistles were blown at such a level that the summer dawning was cast into a vibrant flow of activity.

Factories were broken into; whatever could be used for barricades was hijacked and placed across a street, or a road; trucks, vans, and buses were all commandeered.

Within a matter of hours, entire Nationalist districts were sealed by large groups of young men. The Short Strand and Ardoyne, commandeered buses from the local Corporation Bus Depots. On the Mountpottinger Road, in the Short Strand, several factories were set ablaze sending palls of bellowing black smoke skywards, which could be seen across the city centre. Trucks were taken from the Harkness and Mc Keague's company yards, and *Laverys* Bottling Firm in Seaforde Street, provided crates of bottles for the youths engaging the Saracens that screamed along the roads with a distinctive *whizzing* sound.

The loud thud of rubber bullets broke the air at regular intervals and CS gas drifted ahead of the advancing soldiers of the 2nd Queens, and Parachute Regiment., who eventfully began to fan out into the small close-knit streets of the Short Strand by 7am.

In the near-by Market district, a small group of Official IRA snipers opened fire on soldiers, amid the barricades from Inglis's Bakery.

From the New Lodge district in the north of the city, to the housing estates of Turf Lodge and Ballymurphy in the west, serious rioting had erupted across the Nationalist districts.

The British government had foreseen a degree of opposition and rioting, but nothing on the scale that had erupted and would continue throughout the week. Internment had provoked a surge of resistance within the broad Nationalist community and further estrangement of Nationalists from the governing authorities. Law and any sense of order had broken down amid the working-class Nationalist areas as the Army were now imposing, *"control"* rather than *"order"* on the streets.

Around Ballymurphy and New Barnsley, Paratroopers opened fire and randomly killed civilians, including a priest who was attempting to give the last rites to a dying man.

For those detained, interrogation, or detention awaited in Crumlin Road Gaol. Veteran republican, Jimmy Drumm was taken from his home in Andersonstown along with his son, Sean, and in the back of a Saracen, brought firstly to Shaw's Road, were a convoy of trucks were positioned to convey those arrested, and then to Girdwood Camp.

A local woman challenges troops on the Mountpottinger Road, Short Strand August 1971 [Martin Meyer]

Jimmy had been interned during the war years in *Crumlin Road* and on the *Al Rawdah* prison ship in 1940. He met his wife Marie, a member of Sinn Fein and Cumann Na mBhan, who was visiting republican prisoners in Crumlin Road Gaol in 1942, and they were married upon his release in 1945.

He recalled that they were brought to Girdwood Camp:

"I could hear the barks of Alsatian dogs and the sound of helicopter propellers churning away. I thought we were going to be flown to England. They then assembled us in the camp gymnasium to be processed by RUC Special Branch. There were around 100 men, and I recognised some familiar faces, such as Joe Mc Gurk and Gerry Maguire. The MP's,-[Military Police] would prod you with their batons, shouting obscenities and to move at the double".

The following day, Jimmy and other detainees were brought in batches of six through the back of the Gaol and on to C. Wing. His cell was 15, on C3 along with Liam Sheppard.

D.Wing, 14th July, 2009.
Photo Author

Over the next few days, the internees followed the tradition of electing an O.C and a *"staff"*. Jimmy O'Rawe was the O.C, Billy O'Neill and Art Mc Millen where on the staff, and Jimmy, along with Michael Farrell where in charge of letters and parcels.

The IRA Leadership knew Internment was imminent and had warned most of its key people not to stay in their own homes, which meant that in the initial swoops, the British Army failed to capture their intended targets. Many of those arrested were veteran republicans, Civil Rights activists, and militant opponents of Stormont, along with around 30 IRA Volunteers. *-[Figure of 30 from Joe Cahill, at that time the O.C of the IRA's Belfast Brigade, following Billy Mc Kee's capture by soldiers in Ardoyne in April, 1971]

This was not just Internment of republicans, **it was repression of the *"Nationalist Community"*, on whole, and that was one of the key elements that was to work against its success.** Within, three days of the Internment operation, 22 people had died.

With the Army now controlling streets that were chaotic, everyone was potential to arrest without logic, or reason. One case point of this, among many, is that of James Quinn aged 41, of Thompson Street, Short Strand. He had been protesting to soldiers and the RUC, the day following the introduction of Internment, of inaction at the intimidation of residents by Loyalists, and the wrecking of homes in Bryson Street, a *"mixed"* borderline street between the Nationalist Short Strand and the Unionist streets toward Templemore Avenue.

His persistent protest led to a *"Snatch Squad"* from the Parachute Regiment, trailing him off the Mountpottinger Road, and handing him over to soldiers of 2nd Battalion, Queens Regiment for detention. Mr. Quinn's arrest by the soldiers was photographed by a press photographer, Martin Meyer, from the *Guardian* Newspaper, who on that day was photographing events in the district which had according to the front page of the *Belfast Telegraph* newspaper, saw some of the worst disturbances in the city on Internment Day.

James Quinn was a "Nationalist", not an IRA member, and like many others, that was enough to be sent to Crumlin Road Gaol for six months.

Another story, again one of many, involved a young man called, Joseph Fitzsimons, again who lived in the Short Strand. He was arrested in September 1971 for rioting and sentenced to six months in Crumlin Road Gaol. Joseph was in the IRA and on the day of his release in February 1972, four IRA Volunteers were being buried in his area of Short Strand.

Fellow republican prisoners in the Gaol from that district, and other areas, gave him sympathy cards to bring to the families of the deceased men. Joseph, or *"Joey"*, as he was known, upon arriving back in the district, duly delivered the cards to the families, which he himself would have known.

James Quinn, being taken into Mountpottinger Barracks by a soldier of the 2nd Battalion, Queen's Regiment, following his arrest by Paratroopers. [Martin Meyer]

This done, he then joined the mourners at the funerals of the dead volunteers. In an ironic twist of fate, exactly three months later, Joey, himself was dead, killed in similar circumstances as those he had mourned that February morning, upon leaving *Crumlin Road.*

With events on the ground escalating by the day, the wings of Crumlin Road Gaol began to fill up and, on the 19th September, 88 Internees, including Jimmy Drumm were brought from the Gaol to the football pitch and in batches, flown by Wessex helicopters to Long Kesh Internment Camp. Six warders accompanied each batch of prisoners under armed military guard.

As if in keeping with a crude and draconian tradition, yet another prison ship was moored in Belfast to house any overspill of Internees. The *Maidstone*, followed the *Al Rawdah*, and the *Argenta*. HMS *Maidstone* had been a submarine depot ship that had operated in the Mediterranean during WW11 and had been used as a temporary billet for troops drafted into Belfast since 1969.

Everyone is considered a suspect, Cromac Street, on the 11th August 1971

The Internees were held at the stern of the ship which had been cut open to connect it to another ship, The *Harland Point*. The ship housed 122 Internees in cramped conditions, and when the internees began to be transferred to a new Internment camp at *Magilligan* in January 1972, seven of the prisoners, staged a daring escape through the tight security and evaded capture, despite an intensive Army follow up operation centred on the *Markets* area.

This escape came after several major escapes from Crumlin Road Gaol, in a short period, beginning on the 17th November 1971, when nine republicans escaped from the football pitch, were three months earlier; Wessex helicopters had transported internees to Long Kesh.

Coupled with the events of the 27th June, 1970, in the Ardoyne and Short Strand, Internment was to provide the IRA with a continuous flow of young recruits. It had proven counterproductive and the IRA increased its actions in daily shooting and bomb attacks.

In the four months before Internment-April to July 1971, four British soldiers were killed on active duty; in the four months after Internment being introduced, August to November 1971, thirty soldiers, four UDR and seven RUC members were killed.

This was the cursor of what was to come as 1972 would prove to be the worst year of the conflict with nearly 500 deaths being recorded; 1,382 bomb attacks, and 4,876 people being injured on all sides of the conflict.

As the dark nights of autumn 1971 settled over a city embraced in conflict, the sound of gunfire and the loud *bangs* of the crudely, but lethally made *"Nail Bombs"* was now a familiar sound amid the terrace streets of Belfast's conflict areas.

The IRA was now at war with the British Army. At the end of 1971, the Army calculated that the IRA had fired 17,400 rounds at them and thrown 1,531 Nail Bombs during engagements.

Troops in Seaforde Street, Ballymacarrett-Short Strand

On the weekend of 27th/28th November, the IRA carried out nearly one hundred attacks against troops, buildings and custom huts.

Northern Ireland as a state, stood with its back to the wall, the IRA uprising it had feared since its very foundation, was now a reality, and the Internment policy that Brian Faulkner had been so confident with three months previously in London, had failed.

Loyalist paramilitary groups would also become more involved in the conflict in reaction to the daily IRA bombings and the rising death toll. They would begin a campaign of shootings bombings, and murder against the Nationalist community on whole, justifying their random killings by saying that the Nationalist community was responsible for sheltering and supporting the IRA.

IRA Volunteer 1972

A. Wing-[A.2] Photo 25-6-2009. [Author]

Funeral of Volunteer Gerard Bell, February, 1972, Short Strand

Terrorising a community in a bid to destroy their support for the IRA, proved to be a failed strategy, as Sinn Fein's support in the 1980's/90's grew stronger, rather than decreasing, particularly after it moved toward a political, rather than a military settlement.

The random and at times brutal murders created fear, it did not deter support.

Soldiers line up men on the New Lodge Road in a search operation 1971

Equally, republicans also had to come to the realisation, that *"they were not going to drive the Brits into the sea"* by purely military means and that there needed to be a political strategy that would firstly run parallel with armed struggle, and then in the long term, become the primary tool of struggle.

This became *"The Long War"*.

Republican prisoners were to play an important role in this analysis and debate of future strategy particularly in the eighties.

In May 1972, Billy Mc Kee embarked on a hunger strike in Crumlin Road, to gain political status, [afforded to Internees], for sentenced prisoners. He was joined by other prisoners at various stages to increase the impact of the strike.

Billy McKee in Dublin, 1976

Republican female prisoners in Armagh Gaol also began a hunger strike in supporting the demand, to add to the pressure and create a broad front of protest.

This would stay in tradition with previous campaigns in the Gaol over the decades.

With events on the outside reaching critical and the chance of a ceasefire between Republicans and the British a possibility, the status was granted after 34 days, during which Billy McKee became very ill and had to be moved to the military wing of Musgrave Park Hospital. He recovered and returned to Crumlin Road, and later along with other prisoners moved to Long Kesh Internment camp, until his release in 1975.

Since its inception the Northern Ireland state relied on the use of emergency laws, including widespread powers of arrest and internment to quell republican activity. Corporal punishment such as flogging and birching, [provided for in the Civil Authorities Special Powers Act, 1921] created a backlash of protests, hunger strikes and escapes.

British Army mobile patrol in Ferret Armoured Cars 1973

The prisoners would through each decade resist any attempt to treat them as *"ordinary"*, [ODC's], *"Ordinary Decent Criminals"*, rather than political prisoners.

In 1969, the Northern Ireland prison population was 493; by 1973, it had risen to 3,000, of which 26% were Internees, and the majority of that total were in prison as a direct consequence of the conflict.

Between 1970 - 1975, the British, drawing on tactics in other colonial contexts, used a range of strong-arm tactics, including extra-judicial killings, torture, Internment without trail, and the development of non-jury [Diplock] courts to try those accused of "terrorist offensives".

Paradoxically, however, this security-oriented style afforded de-facto political status to political prisoners and was formalised in 1972 by the republican hunger strike.

Between 9th August 1971 and 5th December 1975, when Internment ended, 1,981 Republicans/Nationalists were interned, along with 107 Loyalists.

Republican prisoners in their analysis and debates in the eighties believed that tactics of whatever aspect were dispensable and worthwhile only insofar as they enhanced the perceived prospects of victory.

A protest over the 1972 Hunger Strike in Crumlin Road Gaol.

Bombing, Shooting Continue

IRA Men End Hunger Strike After Jail Rules Are Eased

BELFAST, June 20 (UPI).—Irish Republican Army men in Belfast's Crumlin Road jail today ended a 36-day hunger strike in return for Britain's virtual concession of political-prisoner status.

In Dublin, a special criminal court freed Joe Cahill, 52, a former commander of the Belfast Provisionals, after finding him innocent of inciting persons to join the IRA, an illegal organization.

Bombing and shooting raged on across Northern Ireland. In Armagh, 35 miles south of Belfast, police overpowered four IRA suspects trying to escape, wounding one of them.

In Belfast, the 31 hunger strikers ended their fast as one of them, the former IRA provisional commander in Belfast Billy McKee, 48, was moved from the jail to a hospital because of his weakened condition.

Rioting erupted in Belfast's Catholic neighborhoods last week when rumors spread that Mr McKee had died. He is halfway through a three-year sentence for illegal possession of arms.

Martin McGuinness, Provisional IRA commander in Londonderry, hailed the outcome of the hunger strike as a victory, especially for Mr. McKee.

A fusillade of gunfire struck the Armagh police headquarters today, and bombs ripped the Town Council building in Strabane, on the Irish Republic border, and a tire firm in Dungannon, 40 miles southwest of Belfast.

The Dungannon bomb, planted by two gunmen, caused no injuries, but two persons were hospitalized after the Strabane explosion, police said.

At least 13 persons suffered injuries in a bombing attack during the night in the predominantly Protestant town of Ballymena, 40 miles north of Belfast, police said.

In Belfast, gunmen ambushed an army patrol in the Catholics' Ardoyne area, wounding six soldiers in a hail of rifle and machine-gun fire, an army spokesman said. One of the troopers died in a hospital, the spokesman said.

The soldier was the fourth British trooper killed in the province in the last 24 hours and the 381st fatality in three years of violence in Northern Ireland.

AP.

Joe Cahill

Retrospective Image

Many republican prisoners regarded tactical eclecticism as vital in advancement, and were pragmatic in approval of new methods. They believed in tactical adaptability.

This grew from the electoral success during the 1981 hunger strike in the H.Blocks of the Maze/Long Kesh prison.

Tradition of inter-movement discipline and unity cohered the bulk of IRA prisoners; tactical initiatives cascade from the leadership, and that inter-movement discipline centralised the movement's political authority. The bulk of activists supported the movement's reorientation throughout the eighties and nineties, although in recent times, some former activists are now beginning to question the nature and ingredient of some policies and how they were directed that led to the final statement in 2007 that *"The war is over"*.

In 1972/73, as more Loyalist prisoners came into Crumlin Road Gaol, Gusty Spence began to analysis the situation among UVF prisoners. Since his imprisonment in 1966, although still a committed Loyalist in every regard, he began to question the sectarian mindset approach.

A Catholic warder, helped get him books, and in particular Irish history books, which he began to read. When young Loyalists came into the Gaol, as part of their de-briefing, he would say: *"Why are you here son?"* What he was trying to do was unlock what motivated them, rather than what they were charged with.

Gusty Spence began to appreciate the importance of education and debate and later in Long Kesh, he tried to instil a military style discipline and routine to keep prisoners focused and motivated, and not succumb to the boredom.

Throughout the mid-late seventies, Crumlin Road Gaol became a volatile environment, as from March 1976, in a change of policy by the British Government in relation to political status, a struggle ensued between prisoners and the administration, over conditions and segregation between republican and Loyalist prisoners held on remand.

Paratroopers at Beechfield Street & Mountpottinger Road junction, Short Strand.

In the late seventies and during the 1980/1981 periods, the Gaol was *filing up*, and conditions became worst; at one point, three prisoners were being allocated to cells, as the back log increased for prisoners on remand.

When prisoners were sentenced and taken to the Maze/Long Kesh prison, republicans went *"On the Blanket"*, a poor, unhealthy existence of sitting naked in a cell, wrapped only in a coarse prison blanket, in lockdown with a comrade, amid *total non-co-operation* with prison regulations, including, *"slop out"*-[removal of toilet needs] in protest at the removal of *"Special Category Status"*, [Political status].

Prisoners refused to leave their cells for toilet and washing, as it often resulted in beatings by the warders, so there was forced removal at various periods to *"hose out"* the cells, often resulting in verbal sectarian and physical brutality of the prisoners.

These cases of brutality implemented by a section, - [Not all], of prison warders against the prisoners, led to the killing of prison officers outside of the prison by the IRA.

In 1978, the British Government was found guilty by the European Court of Human Rights for *"Cruel inhuman, and degrading treatment in the interrogation procedures",* but this had no bearing on British policy toward the republican prisoners.

By December 1979, 370 republican prisoners were *"On the Blanket".*

This protest was to reach its climax in the 1981 Hunger Strike by republican prisoners during which over a period of six months, ten prisoners died, resulting in serious rioting, shootings and bombings, amid protests that attracted world-wide coverage. Thousands of people attended regular protest marches in support of the prisoners as each death, attracted further coverage from the international media, and was further met with increased conflict on the streets.

The *Special Category Status* was eventfully returned to the prisoners in 1983.

In Crumlin Road Gaol, the issue of segregation among Republican and Loyalist prisoners continued into the final years of the Gaol's lifetime. This was mainly centred on remand prisoners on C.Wing and on the 24th November 1991, a republican bomb exploded in the Dining area for C.Wing, killing two Loyalist prisoners; Robert Skey and Colin Caldwell.

The Dining area was a "shared space" between republican and Loyalist prisoners who would rotate eating times to avoid confrontation. But the policy of keeping both sets of prisoners on the same wing was in itself "trouble waiting to happen" and incidents between prisoners, and with staff, increased. Moves to address the issue were implemented, but it took the loss of life to highlight "the obvious".

Crumlin Road Gaol C.Wing, showing all three Landings. Photo, June 2009.
[Author]

In July 1994, Loyalist prisoners, now on A.Wing, staged a protest on the roof of the Gaol, amid rising tensions between Loyalist prisoners and the staff in the Gaol. The roof was damaged and burned in parts, before the protest was brought to an end.

Seventy six years previous, republican prisoners had climbed through on to the roof of A.Wing and flew the Irish flag during protests taking place in B.Wing; in 1994, Loyalist prisoners were back on the roof of A.Wing protesting over conditions in the Gaol; this in its own way, frames the history of conflict in Belfast's Crumlin Road Gaol, the heavy doors of which closed for the final time as a "working prison" in 1996.

CHAPTER 5:
Political Escapes from Belfast Gaol - 1927 - 1972

The first escape of political prisoners from Belfast Gaol did not happen, surprisingly, until 1927. With the end of hostilities in 1924, the vast majority of political prisoners were released. Some were forced to leave the state through deportation to the south or to Britain, others joined the Free State Army through failure to find employment, while there were those who settled back into life in a state that showed them little favour and for which they kept a deep desire to overthrow.

A few unfortunate men remained within the walls of Belfast Gaol among them three Republicans who had been charged with a murder in 1920. Having been tried by a General Court-Martial at Victoria Barracks, Belfast, the three - William Conlon, Francis Boyle and Hugh Rodgers were eventually sentenced to life-imprisonment. Convinced the Northern Ireland government was intent on holding them hostage until they served their full sentences, they decided to escape. Aided in this quest they recruited the help of another prisoner named Edward Thornton and planned their escape for the night of the 9th May 1927.

The prisoners managed to jam the bolt on their cell door, then, after lock-up that night, they carefully opened the door and gained access to the landing. Here, they overpowered the night guard and after tying him up and relieving him of his revolver and keys, they proceeded to let themselves out into the exercise yard. Then with a makeshift rope-ladder, which they had prepared for the escape, they scaled the wall to freedom. A car had been arranged to wait on the Crumlin Road to pick the men up, and with all four escapees on board it sped off in the direction of the city centre via Donegall Street.

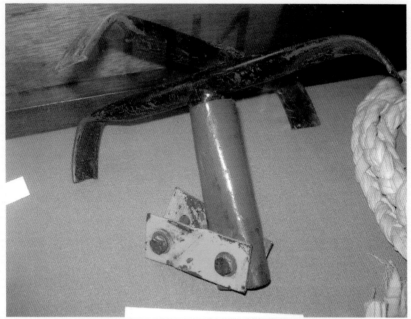

GRAPLING HOOK made in the Gaol. Photo, 26th February 2009. [Author]

A £500.00 reward was issued as the RUC in vain, carried out searches in the Falls Road district in a bid to recapture the four escapees. Two of the four, William Conlon and Edward Thornton were later recaptured, but Francis Boyle and Hugh Rodgers evaded capture and reached Dublin. An extradition bid for their return was refused. Some eleven years later, Internment was re-introduced by the northern authorities with the initial swoops being carried out on Thursday 22nd December 1938 at 04.00. Thirty-four men were detained from the Falls, Ardoyne, Ballymacarrett (Short Strand) and the Dock area and were known Republicans. Before the end of WW11 in 1945, several hundred Republicans would be interned or sentenced in both Belfast and Derry Gaol.

At the beginning, conditions were harsh. All the gains of the past, in terms of being accorded *"Political status"*, mainly for sentenced prisoners were disallowed and had to be fought for again. The food was bad and conditions only improved as a result of hunger strikes and "non-co-operation". The first escape attempt involved a tunnel under the dining hall of C Wing and to drown out the noise of tunneling, regular *singsongs* were held around the manhole that led to the tunnel, but it was soon discovered.

However, with so many Republicans in the Gaol, the desire to escape remained strong and on the 5th June 1941, five Republicans did manage to "*get over the wall*". A lot of thought had gone into the escape and the initial plan was to get as many men out as was possible to do so, but a speedy response by the guards prevented this. The five successful escapees were: Phil Taggart, Liam Burke, Paddy Watson, Eddie Keenan (All from Belfast) and Gerry Doherty from Derry. They had scaled the twenty-foot perimeter wall at a designated point and scrambled down into the grounds of St. Malachy's College before running toward the Crumlin Road.

The men separated in different directions and while three were picked up purely by chance by a friendly doctor in his car close to the Mater Hospital, Eddie Keenan and Gerry Doherty sprinted toward North Queen Street, a Nationalist district some ten minutes' walk from the Gaol. Gerry Doherty ran into the first house he saw with a "Sacred Heart" picture in the window. *"Do you know any Republicans?"* he asked the woman inside. *"Aye, there's one working on the roof now"* she told him. Luck was with them and the men were brought to safe houses where they were kept for over a week before being moved up to the border on the occasion of a major Gaelic football match in Armagh. The escape proved a crucial morale booster for the detainees.

The next major escape from the Gaol came two years later on the morning of Friday January 15th, 1943 and involved the IRA's Chief of Staff, Hugh McAteer from Derry (Who's brother Eddie later became a Nationalist MP), Jimmy Steele former O.C of Belfast, Pat Donnelly from Portadown and Edward (Ned) Maguire. The plan was put together by Hugh Jimmy and Pat with Ned brought in because he was a roof slater by trade.

ROYAL ULSTER CONSTABULARY

REWARD £3,000

The above reward or proportionate amounts thereof will be paid to the person or persons furnishing information to the Police leading to the arrest of any one or more of the persons whose photographs and descriptions are given hereunder and who escaped from Belfast Prison on the morning of 15th January, 1943.

McATEER, Hugh, 76 William Street, Londonderry

STEELE, James, 70 North Queen Street, Belfast

MAGUIRE, Edward, 31 Whiterock Gardens, Belfast

DONNELLY, Patrick, Alexandra Gardens, Portadown

C. G. WICKHAM,
Inspector General.

18th January, 1943.

Wanted Poster, for the 1943, IRA Escapees

Noticing that one could pass from a trapdoor in a top floor toilet into the roof space on A.Wing where the men were housed, they worked for weeks on a scheme which entailed a rope ladder made from bed sheets, a wall hook swathed in bandages and a tall demountable pole, the leather jointing ferrules which had been made in a boot shop in the laundry building.

Gable end of A. Wing, were the IRA prisoners made their escape in January 1943. Photo, June 2008. [Author]

Word of the escape was sent out by a secure "line" in the form of a warder who never was uncovered by the Gaol authorities, to a sweet shop owned by the sisters of prominent Republican Harry White who spent most of his time evading capture. The shop was used to send and receive messages in and out of the Gaol. Unfortunately for the would-be escapers, most of the senior staff still free from internment or capture, were away in Swatragh, County Derry conducting a court-martial of a Belfast man who was a prime suspect for a number of weapon seizures that had occurred in the city.

On the morning of the escape, they separately received permission to go to the washroom, where they broke a hole in the roof and escaped into the exercise yard. From there, they passed over the yard wall fronting the Crumlin Road using the sheet rope to which the bandaged steel crook was attached. *(see rope picture on page 159)* They then dropped to the ground at the gable end of the Warder's Cottages.

It was not as straightforward as it sounds. The demountable pole used for placing the hook upon the barbed wire on top of the wall, was found to be six feet short and Ned Maguire had to stand booted upon Hugh McAteer's shoulders. Hugh was the last to ascend and while the other three had disappeared over the top, Hugh upon making his haul up, lost his grip and fell to the ground. However, he persevered, and with bleeding hands managed to climb over.

The men quickly mingled with the workers walking down the Crumlin Road although they got separated. Jimmy Steele's area of North Queen Street was just under ten minutes' walk away and just like the 1941 escapees; this is where the men headed for. Jimmy, Pat and Ned arrived first and Hugh was guided to safety shortly afterwards, joining the others at Trainor's Scrap Yard in Lancaster Street, where help was found. [1]

Irish News Newspaper report on the IRA escape from the Gaol in January 1943. [Author]

Afterwards, they settled into an empty house, while the biggest security operation in Belfast since 1922 got underway. A £3,000 reward was placed on the heads of the escapees which at that time was a considerable amount of money, but the men were secure within their own community and initial safe houses were found locally and over in Ballymacarrett, while plans were made for further movement, as Ballymacarrett was subject to RUC raids. Both Pat and Ned went south but Jimmy Steele and Hugh McAteer remained in Belfast to help re-organize the IRA. Very few senior men remained free: it was the familiar faces, the hardened young veterans who engaged in the art of survival. Despite this the IRA began to plan a mass break out of prisoners from Derry Gaol and an IRA Army Convention was organized and held in secret in the Ballymacarrett (Short Strand) district of Belfast the following month.

Jimmy Steele in disguise on his Firemans Warrant Card, 1943

The IRA controlled the Auxiliary Fire Service in the Falls district and senior figures from the south notably Charlie Kerins - (Acting Chief of Staff) and Archie Doyle came up to Belfast from Dublin along with others such as Jimmy Clarke from County Donegal and Jim Toner from County Tyrone. The men were quickly put into uniform with proper stamped identity cards complete with authentic photographs taken by a girl in Jerome's, the firm officially appointed for the purpose. They could now relax in reasonable safety, remaining for just under a fortnight in the city. And so it was that the most wanted men in Ireland convened on a winter's day in February 1943 in Belfast's Short Strand area to discuss the critical situation within the Republican movement and the impending escape plan of Republican prisoners from Derry Gaol.

The grim gothic edifice of Derry's Gaol was built on a hill along Harding Street close to the city centre. It housed some 300 internees at the time of the planned escape, taking the overspill from Crumlin Road Gaol. The late Alfie Hanaway of Belfast remembered as a sixteen-year-old Fianna member (IRA Youth Wing) who had been arrested for drilling at the top of the Whiterock Road, being dispatched there as a young internee in 1940. He recalled "*going down*" into the cells as if underground, which to an extent, it was. Standing in the cell for the first time feeling isolated and probably somewhat apprehensive of what lay ahead of him, he heard voices with Belfast accents. He pulled a table over on which to stand, in an endeavour to reach the window, then, no sooner was he on top of it, he felt himself being aggressively hauled to the ground by two warders and warned "*not to do that again*". Young Alfie was later removed to the prison ship "*Al Rawdah*" and then to Crumlin Road Gaol. [2]

The Derry escape operation had begun in November 1942 when Billy Graham of Belfast had started a tunnel from under the floorboards of his cell with Harry O'Rawe and Jimmy O'Hagan in support. They had to sink a fifteen-foot vertical shaft before burrowing a tunnel eighty feet long. The excavation was carried out at night and while two of the men tunnelled, the third kept watch for the night patrols who flashed their torches on the bunk beds to satisfy themselves that no prisoner was missing. As soon as the man on watch heard the patrol, he would signal the two men below who shinned up the rope and jumped into bed covering up their clothes.

The tunnel had been propped up in places by boards and sandbags made from pillowcases filled with soil and was for "*bellying through*", being too narrow to turn in. The clay removed from it, some fifteen tons, was placed under cells, flushed down manholes, or discreetly scattered on soil beds in the yard. They worked with the aid of candles made from salvaged cooking fat, carried on small tin lids. When the candle, through lack of oxygen went out, the men knew it was time to come up out of the tunnel.

The late Harry White takes up the story:

"There was little we on the outside could do to help other than direct them towards the Logue's house (point of exit) in Harding Street, giving them a fix upon a tall chimney behind it. Paddy Adams, uncle of Gerry Adams, who was O.C in the prison, could signal and receive directions at a high window from Liam Burke on the outside - (himself still at large after his escape from Belfast Gaol in 1941). Liam Burke who had been imprisoned within the Gaol previously knew the layout well and had chosen Logue's as the place for the tunnel to surface.

In their "touch and go" passage they suffered everything: a roof collapse which temporarily trapped Billy Graham, a flood of underground water which had to be bailed out and then plugged, and most unsettling of all, a well-preserved coffin which had to be circumvented by digging underneath it. Some of the men fainted on the final morning as they bellied through the suffocating passage and had to be dragged along by their preceding comrade. Finally, early on Sunday morning, the 20th

March 1943, twenty-one young men poked their way upwards through the small coal shed of the Logue's at 15 Harding Street off Abercorn Road just south-east of the old prison, passing through their small kitchen, much to the stunned astonishment of the startled family."

Waiting to pick the men up were Jimmy Steele and Liam Burke in a furniture van which had been driven from Belfast the previous day and parked in Abercorn Place. Shortly after 8.30 am the first of the muddied men came sprinting down the short residential street, down a flight of steps and over to where the van was parked followed by twenty others. As fast as the van could make up speed, the escapees made haste toward the Donegal border and freedom.

The Derry escape was a great morale boost for a Republican movement already under pressure both north and south but had little impact other ways as once again the De Valera regime moved against the movement and arrested the escapees. Hugh McAteer was particularly galled by the arrest of the majority of the Derry escapees in Donegal that evening by Free State soldiers. He remarked, *"The southern government is co-operating with the British. Internees guilty of no crime are imprisoned in what is supposed to be the sympathetic south."*

Jimmy Steele, in later life

By the end of April 1943, only three of the twenty-one from the Derry escape were still at liberty. Edward - (Ned) Maguire, who had escaped from Belfast Gaol three months previously, was arrested by Gardai in County Donegal and sent to the

Curragh Internment Camp. Sean Hamill from Belfast, one of the Derry escapees was arrested in Dublin while the following month Jimmy Steele was captured when 70 RUC personal sealed off Amcomri Street in the Beechmount area of the Falls Road. Just two days earlier, RUC tenders backed by British soldiers had sealed-off the street in a raid whilst Harry White and Jimmy Trainor were staying there. This prompted both men to move houses and Harry moved over to a safe house in Seaforde Street in Ballymacarrett which he had previously used.

Liam Burke and Alfie White, who had escaped from Derry, were captured when a house that they were staying at in a Unionist district of South Belfast, was raided at Easter

On August 3rd, 1943 heavy prison sentences were imposed by Lord Justice Murphy, a member of the Orange Order and the Black Preceptory [and the man who sentenced Tom Williams to be executed the previous year] , on eleven IRA volunteers including Jimmy Steele and Liam Burke. Before the sentences were handed down, Jimmy Steele said: *"I have nothing to say because I do not recognize the right of Lord Justice Murphy to judge me."*

In Belfast Gaol in July 1943 there were 200 sentenced Republican prisoners on A.Wing with Patrick McCotter as O.C with about the same number of Republican internees in D.Wing.

Hugh McAteer was arrested in Crocus Street in the early afternoon of Saturday November 21st 1943 having just left St. Paul's Church on the Falls Road. He walked into a dragnet of RUC Special Branch men and would spend the next seven years in Belfast Gaol's A.Wing.

On release from Belfast Gaol Republicans found a movement in financial and organizational ruin although as has always been the case, it tended to spring back into functional mode and reorganize to a capability that was always a threat to the northern Unionist government. The Special Powers Act remained on the Statue Book and internment was introduced again on the 21 December 1956 just ten days after the IRA had launched its *"Border Campaign"*.

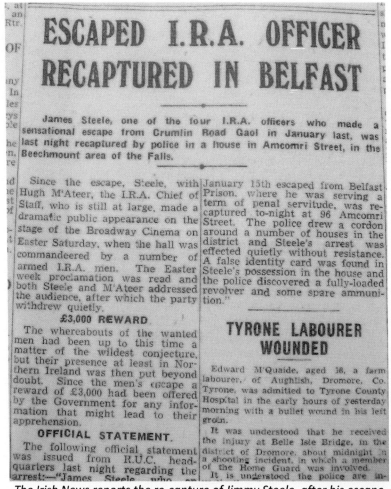

ESCAPED I.R.A. OFFICER RECAPTURED IN BELFAST

James Steele, one of the four I.R.A. officers who made a sensational escape from Crumlin Road Gaol in January last, was last night recaptured by police in a house in Amcomri Street, in the Beechmount area of the Falls.

Since the escape, Steele, with Hugh M'Ateer, the I.R.A. Chief of Staff, who is still at large, made a dramatic public appearance on the stage of the Broadway Cinema on Easter Saturday, when the hall was commandeered by a number of armed I.R.A. men. The Easter week proclamation was read and both Steele and M'Ateer addressed the audience, after which the party withdrew quietly.

£3,000 REWARD.

The whereabouts of the wanted men had been up to this time a matter of the wildest conjecture, but their presence at least in Northern Ireland was then put beyond doubt. Since the men's escape a reward of £3,000 had been offered by the Government for any information that might lead to their apprehension.

OFFICIAL STATEMENT.

The following official statement was issued from R.U.C. headquarters last night regarding the arrest:—"James Steele who

January 15th escaped from Belfast Prison, where he was serving a term of penal servitude, was recaptured to-night at 96 Amcomri Street. The police drew a cordon around a number of houses in the district and Steele's arrest was effected quietly without resistance. A false identity card was found in Steele's possession in the house and the police discovered a fully-loaded revolver and some spare ammunition."

TYRONE LABOURER WOUNDED

Edward M'Quaide, aged 18, a farm labourer, of Aughlish, Dromore, Co. Tyrone, was admitted to Tyrone County Hospital in the early hours of yesterday morning with a bullet wound in his left groin.

It was understood that he received the injury at Belle Isle Bridge, in the district of Dromore, about midnight in a shooting incident, in which a member of the Home Guard was involved. It is understood the police are in-

The Irish News reports the re-capture of Jimmy Steele, after his escape in January 1943. *[Author]*

Once more what was regarded as *"rights"* to decent treatment, last won by hunger strikes and attitudes of non-co-operation, from 1938-1945, were not automatically accorded. They had to be fought for yet again. Internment entailed the same mixture of frustration and boredom with hardships for dependents. However, escape was the predominant thought in many minds. Gerry Maguire, then 25 years of age and interned in C3, describes an attempt at tunnelling, in which he was an active participant.

The tunnel went from D1, opposite the room where the PO, Johnny Smith was and in 12 months of tunnelling Johnny never knew a thing about it. Three shifts a day, regular as clockwork. It began as a hole in the wall into the ventilation shaft and then down and along. We had gone 90 feet and were just over half way complete when the tunnel was accidentally discovered. A "screw" (warder) happened to knock against the mirror on the wall which concealed the entry hole and the game was up! Four men were discovered in the tunnel and locked in a cell to await a beating. We discovered this and broke down the cell door with a crowbar which one of our men had concealed in his mattress (most of the tools had been obtained from workmen doing repairs in the prison) and rescued them. Then we returned to our cells with hostages. After a" parley", we released the hostages unharmed on the understanding that there would be no reprisals and no loss of privileges. However, the next day, 15th March, 1958, a force of "Commandos" (Special riot police) came, six into every cell and beat up everyone. We didn't have a chance. One Lurgan man in C.Wing got a broken leg and broken ribs. Frank Card, and Billy O'Neill were also injured.

In another reference to this escape written from a pro-prison perspective, the attempted escape is documented as leading out of the first cell on C1 and was discovered while the internees were off the wing on exercise during an inspection after suspicion was aroused by more than the normal activity around the cell. The tunnel ran close to D.Wing and toward the perimeter wall and it was claimed to be 45 feet long when discovered. No mention is made of the beatings afterwards.

Another reference to the escape states it led from Frank Card's, [Proinsias Mac Art] cell on D1, which ties in with Gerry Maguire's account of the tunnel.

[Both these men, would later be involved in the 1972 Hunger Strike in the Gaol in May-June, 1972]

The memories of the 1957-1961 period are all not grim. Some recall the "*Ghost of D Wing*" with a smile and again involved a tunnel. An Armagh man had been tunnelling and emerged covered in dirt. The next day the papers reported a warder swearing that he had seen an apparition!

The next escape was to occur on *Boxing Day* [26 December] 1960 when the majority of the internees had all been released due to the "*fizzling out*" of the border campaign. However sentenced prisoners were still being held on A.Wing and it was two of these who made the break to freedom. John Kelly from 12 Adela Street off the Antrim Road [just a few minutes' walk from the prison] and Daniel Donnelly from Omagh made their escape in the old-fashioned manner by lowering themselves down a seventy-foot makeshift rope having removed the bars from Kelly's cell on A2 with a reliable hacksaw blade, which was never recovered.

The hacksaw blades were smuggled into the Gaol in a basket of fruit.

Under the cover of sleet showers, they avoided the probing searchlights and made their way across the yard to the wall beside the warder's cottages. Here they threw the rope up and secured it to the top of the wall by means of a hook. Donnelly went up and over the wall first and dropped into a passageway behind the houses. John Kelly followed, but as he attempted to reach the top of the wall, the rope snapped sending him hurtling back toward the ground breaking his ankle in the process. Dan Donnelly having realized that something had happened to Kelly proceeded out on to the Crumlin Road and headed briefly to Kelly's house as the alarm had now been raised. John Kelly's parents knew of the escape and having provided Donnelly with clothes, had him quickly moved to another house. He was then taken from the area by Republicans and after being laid up in a Furniture removal yard which was closed for the Christmas period, he was eventually brought into County Monaghan. John Kelly was charged with attempting to escape and had any privileges removed. He was not released until 1963. Six years later at the outbreak of the recent conflict, John Kelly was to the fore of the Citizens Defence Committees set up following the 1969 pogrom and in turn the new Provisional movement.

The last internee of the period was released from the prison on the 25th April 1961.

Within a matter of eight years the north had erupted into street warfare as the Unionist state found itself reeling from its own blatant discrimination of its Nationalist citizens. Britain had been forced by events to intervene and thousands of British troops were now on the streets. A new and more potent IRA had emerged whose role was turning from defensive to offensive action against the state and the British Army.

Stormont once more turned to its old tool of oppression, Internment. But unlike previous occasions in the history of the state, the RUC was not strong enough to implement the policy and it was left to the British Army who were to the fore as the primary force in the war against the IRA. So once again with the support of Whitehall in London, Internment would be used to suppress the Nationalist community.

So it was that on Monday 9th August 1971 at 04.00am, 3,000 British troops swooped on Nationalist areas throughout the north mainly in Belfast, Armagh and Derry. However, the *Unionist Panacea* as the British General Officer commanding in the north, General Tuzo referred to it, was failing as the raids sparked off a reaction of full-scale resistance never experienced in the history of the northern state.

Doors of homes were broken down and men, young and old were dragged from their beds. Women were verbally abused and the cry of children ignored as fathers and husbands were pushed into the back of a waiting Saracen armoured car en-route to an interrogation centre, the main one in Belfast being Girdwood Army camp close to the Crumlin Road Gaol.

Women and girls formed up amid the terrace streets, banging dustbin lids, a crude but effective signalling system which echoed across the back-to-back houses with a high-pitched shrill, while whistles were blown as such a level that the summer dawning was cast into a vibrant flow of activity. Factories were broken into and trucks, vans and buses were used for barricades. The Short Strand, Ardoyne and Upper Falls districts where the Corporation bus depots were located, were heavily barricaded in by the commandeered buses. By late morning as the soldiers began to break through and try to establish a foothold, CS gas drifted across their advance as the loud thud of rubber bullets filled the air at regular intervals. Crates of bottles littered the streets as Saracen APC'S (Armoured Personnel Carrier) screamed toward battling rioters followed by soldiers on foot firing rubber bullets. Gunfire blended into the rioting as IRA snipers and soldiers exchanged fire amid the chaos. Black smoke bellowed into the clear morning sky from the burning buildings as **Operation Demetrius** the British Army codename for the operation, launched Belfast into the worst conflict the city had witnessed since 1921.

Internment was failing in its objective of breaking the IRA; the old weapon of the state was proving disastrous. By the 12th August the death toll since internment morning of the 9th, had risen to twenty-two killed as gun battles swept the Nationalist areas of Belfast and Derry. Fifteen had been killed on internment day, thirteen of whom were killed by the British Army. Six, all innocent civilians, were shot dead by troops in the Whiterock/New Barnsley area. Two other men shot by troops nearby in Ballymurphy died of their wounds before the month ended, bringing the death toll for the three days to 24 dead; men and women. Internment had provoked a surge of

Sean Mac Staifion alongside Martin Meehan, who escaped from Crumlin Road Gaol, in December 1971

resistance and a further estrangement of the Nationalist community from the governing authorities, in Stormont and Westminster.

Law and any sense of order had broken down within the working-class Nationalist areas. Intimidation was widespread along the borderline areas and thousands of people were forced to flee their homes. The death toll began to escalate. It was against this background that internees began to flood into C.Wing along with sentenced prisoners into B. Wing [later to become the loyalist wing during that period].

Despite the heavy presence of British troops throughout Belfast, the Internment period became notable for the number of escapes successfully affected by Republican prisoners. Escape committees both inside and outside the prison were busy in planning and organizing the escapes. But if an opportunity presented itself, individual initiative kicked in and a prisoner made good his escape such as was the case involving Sean Hanna from Henrietta Street in the Market District, who managed to walk out the front gate in 1971 despite all the security. During November/December of the same year, twelve Republicans escaped in what are now folk-lore stories and well documented.

On the 17th November, nine Republican prisoners being held on remand went over the wall from the football pitch through the already cut barbed wire perimeter and into waiting cars. Seven were successful escaping to the south, but two, Christopher Keenan from Anderson Street, Short Strand and Daniel McMullan from Oakfield

Street, Ardoyne, were later captured. After this escape, they closed the prison down for two weeks while army engineers moved in to make the prison more secure. They erected barbed wire and corrugated iron fences all around the pitch to prevent access toward the perimeter wall which in turn had armed soldiers in the watch towers. [3]

However, this did not prevent the escape of three more Republicans [Martin Meehan, Tony "*Dutch*" Doherty and Hugh McCann] escaping on the 2nd December during a Gaelic football match. In a planned operation they squeezed into a manhole having covered themselves in butter to help against the winter cold and stayed there cramped, cold and wet for five hours emerging at 6pm. Under the cover of thick fog, they managed to escape over the wall with a makeshift rope, dropping down into an alleyway between Clifton Park Avenue and the Gaol. Still evading the notice of the British Army sentries, they sprinted to a waiting car, which Martin Meehan had arranged to be left in Clifton Park Avenue. Their escape route took them down Agnes Street on to the Shankill Road, before cutting through on to the Falls Road and into McDonnell Street and safety. Martin Meehan crossed the border that Sunday and continued his involvement in IRA operations along the border from Dundalk. He was recaptured in Jamaica Street in the Ardoyne nine months later on the 9th August 1972. Hugh McCann was recaptured in Andersonstown in May 1971.

Tunnels continued to occupy the men's time and C.Wing was the center point of digging in 1972, although a more direct approach was taken in February 1972, when 85 Republican remand prisoners on C.Wing, having taken control of the wing, tried to break out en-masse only to be halted by British soldiers who threatened to shoot the first prisoner to cross the exercise yard wall.

Three months later, Michael Willis, aged 19, from Belfast and a member of the Official IRA, [just as Sean Hanna did] walked out the front gate on the 5th May despite the heavy security. Willis had been sentenced to ten years on *a firearms charge* and was eventually after a week, picked up by the IRA who smuggled him over the border and on to Dublin.

That same month, on the 15th, Republican sentenced prisoners embarked on a hunger strike led by their O.C, Billy Mc Kee, to win the right of political Status again.

One of those on the strike, Robert Campbell from the New Lodge area, was moved to the Mater hospital on the 6th June due to the condition of his health. The IRA quickly moved, and removed him from the hospital the following day.

Rope made from bed sheets.
Photo, 26th February, 2009. [Author]

The hunger strike lasted for 36 Days, and amid an upsurge of shooting and riots in Nationalist districts and with secret talks attempting to bring about a ceasefire, the prisoners had their demands met for political recognition.

Two Loyalist prisoners, Danny Strutt and Tommy Cull, also escaped from Crumlin Road during this period.

Tommy Cull from Danube Street, Belfast was 21 years of age and a bricklayer by trade.

Both and he and Danny-[James] Strutt, were members of the Shankill Road's, UVF A.Company and had been jailed, along with two other men for six years on charges of armed robbery.

1971, Loyalist Excape

Cull took the place of another prisoner due for release and managed to walk through the *"Air-Lock"* and then the main gate at the beginning of October, 1971.

Danny Strutt, [*James*, as in his picture which appeared in local newspapers at the time], followed Cull some twenty five days later.

Strutt, aged 31, came from Bootle Street, Belfast.

There were two versions circulating at the time of how he managed to escape; the version of him sawing through window bars and then scaling a wall-[which would have been covered with barbed wire and floodlights, and watched over by armed soldiers], was the one that was promoted as the *true version.*

Republican prisoners achieved scaling the walls in November 1971, so it is viable.

Another version, that cannot be substantiated, is that he was provided with a warder's uniform, enabling him *to walk out* of the Gaol.

This was rejected by Loyalists, who claim there was no *"inside help".*

Whatever, version is to be taken with credence, *he escaped!*

Danny Strutt was re-captured a year later in Larkhill, Scotland while involved in stealing explosives from a quarry. He was returned to the north and later was the UVF O.C. in Compound 18 at Long Kesh, before his release.

Another Loyalist attempt to escape involved a tunnel in the basement, directly under what was the condemned cell at the bottom of C.Wing. A tunnel leading from a cell on the same wing, was also detected and shut down.

Some prisoners such as republican prisoner Danny Keenan from Derry escaped more than once. Having escaped from Crumlin Road Gaol on 13th January 1973, following recapture, he later escaped from Magilligan prison in 1975. Another, was Jim Bryson, an IRA Volunteer from Ballymurphy. He was one of seven republicans who had escaped on the 17th February 1971 from HMS *Maidstone*, a WW11 submarine supply ship, which was being used as a temporary facility to house republican internees at Belfast Harbour, Bryson was recaptured by the British Army in the Falls area, eight months later, and found himself in Crumlin Road Gaol.

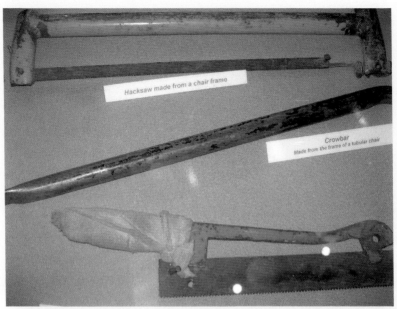

Tools made to aid an escape. Photo, 26th February, 2009. [Author]

Crumlin Road Gaol, the tunnel leading to the Courthouse.
Photo: October, 2004. [Author]

On the morning of 22nd February, 1973, Jim Bryson and fellow republican, Malachy Mc Carey, were being escorted through the Gaol tunnel toward the courthouse, when they overpowered the warders *at gunpoint*, taking their uniforms.

They then proceeded toward the court, were Jim Bryson scaled a back wall and failing to steal a car, set off on foot toward Unity Flats. Malachy Mc Carey was recognized as he attempted to walk out the front entrance of the heavily guarded court house, and detained. Meanwhile, Jim Bryson reached the safety of Unity Flats, where he was quickly taken to a safe house, while the British Army began searching the immediate area, including the Unity flats complex.

As in his first escape, Jim Bryson, who was high on the British Army *wanted list,* evaded capture, and after a period of time in the south, was active again in Belfast.

At around, 6.35pm, on the evening of Friday, 31st August, 1973, six months after his daring escape, 25-year-old, Jim Bryson, along with three other volunteers; Patrick Mulvenna, James O'Rawe, and Frank Duffy, were travelling in a car in the Ballymurphy estate, when two soldiers of the 3rd Battalion, Royal Green Jackets, operating a covert surveillance *hide* in a vacant flat on Glenallina Road, opened fire on the car on the Ballymurphy Road, having observed rifles pointing out of the windows.

One of the soldiers, a Lance/Corporal, was a marksman, and he hit both Jim Bryson and Patrick Mulvenna. James O'Rawe was wounded in the shoulder, and along with Frank Duffy, quickly captured.

Jim Bryson, who was seriously wounded, later died of his wounds on the 2nd September.

The *Green Jackets,* would have viewed the removal of Jim Bryson, a determined, and audacious volunteer, with some satisfaction, while his death would have been viewed as a great loss to the IRA, particularly in Belfast.

He had been involved in numerous actions against troops and showed an almost reckless, if not arrogant, daring at times.

Patrick Mulvenna, was 19 years of age and came from a family of republicans; his father had been interned, and his brothers and sister were also imprisoned.

James O'Rawe, was also a well-known republican, whose family connections to the Republican Movement went back to the war years, as was Frank Duffy, who had been in the south with Jim Bryson.

Another escape from the Gaol involving guns, took place, nine years later on the 10th June, 1981, when eight republican prisoners made yet another escape, which ranked as audacious, and daring as any of those previous escapes in 1971.

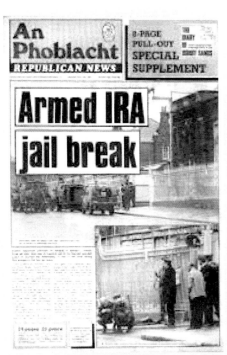

The story of this escape *has been well documented* and joins the long list of escapes that took place from the *"Crum"*, over the years that saw 37 republicans, and two Loyalists make *"the break for freedom"*.

GAOL ESCAPE PAPER

NOTES:

1: Trainor's Scrapyard in Lancaster Street was the same location used by the IRA's Ballymacarrett Company in July 1935, when as the stand-by Company they had to defend the area during a breakout of sectarian violence over the 12th period.

The Trainor's were republicans from the Dock's area of Belfast.

2: Interview with historian Sean O'Coinn,1998.

3: On Friday 19th November, 1971, soldiers from 45 Royal Marine Commando based in Belfast, moved into the small quiet village of Portglenone and along with the RUC sealed off the village They carried out searches of the Cistercian *"Our Lady of Bethlehem"* *monastery* and the wooded area close by.

The raids were in connection to the escape from the Gaol and the re-capture of Christopher Keenan and Danny Mullan near Omagh. When the car they were travelling in was stopped, both men were apparently dressed as priests and a monk and a lay preacher were also in the car.

At around the same time, two other escapees were being smuggled over the border to join five others already in the south.

Three other men, from Omagh, Portglenone and Toomebridge were later arrested, but released on bail, in connection to aiding the escapees.

A. Wing-[A.2] Photo, June 2009. [Author]

Soldiers man a VCP outside Crumlin Road Gaol 1981

CHAPTER 6:
STAFF, ADMINISTRATION & THE BRITISH ARMY.

In any story there are always two sides to be told. While the Gaol and its history mainly focuses on the experience of the men incrassated, whether sentenced or interned, there is another story, one *"from the other side"* that needs to be acknowledged for a proper and authentic account to be written.

In any profession, there are good and bad, just as in conflict, suffering is not reserved to one side, or the other. The pain of loss affects us all the same; the human dimension knows no barrier.

A nineteenth century Warder in Crumlin Road Gaol

Warders, Prison Officers, or *"Screws"* as they were commonly known had the job of *"Hands On"* administration, and its legacy is one that most probably deserves a more in-depth analysis. It had its success and failure and the men who filled the ranks of the *Staff*, ranged from the very decent, to the shameful. *Some* were even outright sectarian in their mind-set.

Following the end of WW1 and the subsequent shortage of work, it was natural for some servicemen to find employment in the Prison and Police service.

In those times wages and conditions fell far short of those enjoyed by later employees in the service. The cottages still evident to this day at the front of the Gaol were used as accommodation for staff beginning in the mid-twenties.

In 1920, a Governor's salary was £350 per year, [In England, it was £600}, his Deputy earned £150 per year, as did the Medical Officer and the Prison Chaplin.

A similar pattern in recruitment developed after the end of WW11, but it was not until the

A Prisoner in the Gaol Garden with three Warders. Late 1940's - Post WW11 [Author]

late forties that working conditions significantly improved for prison staff.

Just as the internees formed clubs in the Gaol in the forties, likewise the warders had their various associations, such as wartime veterans of the Royal Ulster Rifles.

Early picture of Gaol Staff line up.

In 1943 following the IRA escape of January 1943, several republican prisoners on A.Wing from where the escape took place, later accounted experience of deliberate ill-treatment from warders.

Some believed that the worst kind were assigned to duty on A.Wing and would show little compunction in using their batons at any sign of non-co-operation from prisoners.

Complaints of miss- treatment were often ignored by the Governor and disciplinary action was over used for even trivial offensives.

Billy Mc Kee recalled his first term of imprisonment in the Gaol during the forties period and commented how punishment was almost implemented on a daily basis; *"You could be punished for almost anything and nothing".*

Food was always a contentious issue in the Gaol, but in A.Wing it was particularly bad, often cold and under cooked. Even complaints over this could result in some form of punishment being implemented.

This policy appeared to be reserved for republican sentenced prisoners, while in the main the internees were left alone and their full political status recognised.

ELS 1950 inscription on a wall. Photo, June 2009. [Author].

Another form of punishment that was highly controversial yet used by the northern administration, was the use of the *"Cat"* and the *"Birch"* to whip prisoners. Of the two, the Birch could be the worst.

This punishment was laid down during sentence by the judge and would be carried out in the Gaol at a time of the Governor's choosing.

A prisoner would be brought underground to the boiler house and in the presence of the Governor and a medical officer, the man would be whipped, each stroke counted out by the Governor. The medical officer was present simply to ensure the victim did not suffer any heart failure during the procedure.

Such brutality came as the *"norm"* during that period, but in the later history of the Gaol during the recent conflict, retaliation against prison officers particularly by the IRA was inevitable.

The actions of those warders, or prison officers to use the modern terminology, who melted out physical or sectarian verbal abuse, resulted in prison officers who in the main, were simply doing what they considered a job of work, becoming targets of retaliatory action outside the Gaol.

In total, twenty-seven prison officers were killed during the conflict, including two women who were warders in the Women's Gaol in Armagh.

Others, outside of Crumlin Road, were based in the H.Blocks of the Maze-[Long Kesh] Prison, were republican prisoners suffered brutality for non-co-operation during the *"Blanket Protest"* of the late seventies to have political status restored. This status was removed by the British Government in 1976 after the closure of the Long Kesh Internment camp and the building of the new H.Blocks close by, now renamed the Maze Prison.

We are mainly focusing on those who were serving in Crumlin Road, but have also made reference to those who were working at the Maze/Long Kesh prison.

The first prison officer killed was on the 23rd September, 1974, when Senior Officer William Mc Cully, aged 58 was shot by the IRA. He had joined the prison service in September 1948 and had 23 years' service when he retired in 1971.

He was working as a school caretaker and was shot at his home.

Less than two years later, John Cummings, aged 55, who was working as a Clerk in the Gaol was shot by the IRA at his home in Dunmurray, Belfast on the 19th April, 1976.

The next serving officer in the *Crum* to be killed, again by the IRA, was John Milliken, aged 57 who held the rank of Principle Officer. He had seventeen years' service, having joined in July 1960. He was shot as he travelled home on the 22nd June, 1977.

John Milliken was one of three killed that year, the other two were working at Magilligan and the Maze. Principle Officer Desmond Irvine aged 38 was the Secretary of the Prison Officers Association and had been in the service since September 1964. He was serving in the Maze Prison when he was shot by the IRA on the 7th October, 1977.

His brother also worked in the prison service.

The following month, the IRA took retaliation for the situation in the H.Blocks when it struck at the very top of the prison service by shooting the Governor of the Maze at his home on the 26th November, 1978.

Albert Miles, aged 50, had joined the prison service in October 1958 and had worked there for twenty years. [He would be the first of two Maze Governor's to be shot by the IRA]

Three weeks later, another prison clerk in *Crumlin Road*, John Murdie Mc Tier, died when the car he was driving out of the Gaol on the 14th December was fired on by the IRA. Two other prison officers in the car as passengers were injured.

The following year, 1979 with the volatile situation in the H Blocks reaching critical, the IRA stepped up the shooting of prison staff. That year, seven were killed that included the Assistant Governor of Crumlin Road Gaol, Edward Jones and three senior officers.

The first fatality was Patrick Mackin, a retired Principle Officer who was shot by the IRA in his home along with his wife, on the 3rd February, 1979.

The couple lived in the Oldpark Road area of Belfast.

Patrick Mackin, who was a Catholic, joined the prison service in August 1951 and had served for over 27 years until his retirement in November 1978.

He also worked in the prison service college and his son was a serving member of the RUC.

Another Catholic prison officer who was working in *Crumlin Road* was Michael Cassidy.

Born on the 27th May, 1948 in Augher County Tyrone, Michael Cassidy moved to Belfast in the late sixties where he met his wife. They married in 1971.

He joined the prison service in February 1973 and he was shot by the IRA leaving St. Macartan's Cathedral, in Clogher, County Tyrone where he was attending his sister's wedding along with his wife, on the 16th April, 1979.

At the time of his death he was living in the Antrim Road area of North Belfast and had two children.

In September, the staff in the Gaol lost two more of its members within a week, one of whom was the Assistant Governor as the IRA continued to hit the echelons of the prison service at every level.

The first shooting occurred on the 14th September, when George Foster aged 30, and two colleagues came under fire from the IRA as they were driving into the prison.

Mr. Foster died in the attack and one of his colleagues was injured.

Five days later on the 19th September, the staff at the Gaol were left in shock when Assistant Governor Edward Jones aged 60, was shot by the IRA as he sat in his car at traffic lights on the Crumlin Road about 100 yards from the Gaol.

Edward Jones originated from Newtownbutler, County Fermanagh where he was born in 1919, just as the war of Independence was beginning. His Father had fought in WW1.

At the age of seventeen in 1935, Edward joined the Army, serving in the Irish Guards. He served during WW11, during which time, he married his wife Dorothy, who's Father had been an officer in the Grenadier Guards. He had died at a young age, 32 years old, through illness when Dorothy was only ten years of age.

Door leading into Administration Block, Crumlin Road Gaol.
17th October, 2004. [Author]

After the war, Edward Jones joined the prison service in March 1946 and continued working there until his death in 1979. He was due to retire within a few months of his shooting.

In October 1977, the family home was attacked in Carrickfergus when a bomb destroyed the front of the house, but none of the family where injured. Edward Jones was buried from his home at Jellicoe Park to Carnmoney cemetery and was survived by his wife and ten children.

In November, as the year was coming to a close, the IRA struck once more at those working in the Gaol. On the 5th of the month they shot Thomas Gilhooley, aged 25 while he was sitting in his car at road traffic lights, then two days later, the INLA shot David Teeney, also aged 25, who worked as a Clerk in the Gaol.

Both men had been in the prison service for only a few years.

David Teeney's shooting was quickly followed by the shooting of three more prison officers; two from Crumlin Road and one, Gerald Melville, who worked at the Maze/Long Kesh prison.

Gerald Melville, aged 45, had joined the prison service in February 1964 and was shot by the IRA on the 23RD November, while Chief Officer William Wright, aged 58 and Senior Officer William Wilson, were both killed in December.

William Wright had joined the prison service in February 1947 and had survived a previous attempt on his life in 1977. The IRA shot him on the evening of the 3rd December as he parked his car in the driveway of his home.

At the time of his death, he was the Chief Warder in Crumlin Road Gaol.

While the IRA continued to target those who worked in the Maze and Magilligan, two other members of the prison service who worked at Crumlin Road Gaol were shot and killed by Loyalist Paramilitaries; William Burns and James Peacock.

William Burns, aged 45 was shot outside his home at 7am in Knocknagoney Park in east Belfast on the 30th December, 1980, by a group calling itself The *Loyalist Prisoner's Action Force*. It claimed he was shot in retaliation for the *"maltreatment of Loyalist prisoners"*.

Old Laundry Building

The grim facade of the Gaol. April 2009. [Author].

Another prison officer was shot and wounded shortly afterwards the same morning at Castlereagh Street, also in east Belfast.

Mr.Burns was a member of the Orange Order's Ballymacarrett Lodge, 1053.

James Peacock was 44 years of age and married with five children. Originally from Liverpool, he was fatally injured when the UVF forced their way into his home at Joanmount Park in north Belfast, on the night of Wednesday, 1st September, 1993 and shot him. He died an hour after being rushed to hospital.

Mr.Peacock was on long term sick leave at the time of the shooting.

His killing came after a UVF statement threatened to kill more prison officers due to trouble that had broken out in the Loyalist wing at the Maze Prison.

The IRA continued to target those who worked at the Maze/Long Kesh Prison.

Among those killed was another Governor of the prison, William Mc Connell, who was shot at close range at his home in the Belmont suburb of east Belfast on the 6th March, 1984. He had joined the prison service in September 1971.

At the time of his killing, he was the Deputy Governor in charge of security at the Maze.

An IRA statement in claiming responsibility, said that he had: "*organized and directed beatings*" in the prison.

There were periods in the history of Crumlin Road Gaol when political conflict was not the dominating factor such as the post-war years from 1945 to 1957 and the years following the end of a third Internment period, from 1961 to 1970.

The "Domestic" aspect of the Gaol differed little from other prisons in that prisoners were tasked with different work roles such as working in the kitchens, Wood yard, Shoe shop, Garden, or Laundry. The old Laundry building was situated between the Crumlin Road side of A.Wing and the Warder's cottages, and the Garden was located at the rear of the Gaol behind the prison hospital.

The Prison Staff Cottages 1953. [Author]

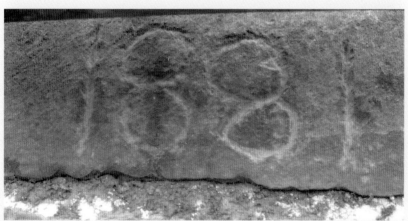

1881 inscribed on the wall at the back north-east corner, 2008. [Author].

Over the lifetime of the Gaol, seventeen men were executed by hanging and their bodies buried within the prison walls in unconsecrated ground; the only mark of burial being the man's initials scratched into the wall against the year of execution.

When Charles Lanyon first designed the Gaol, a gallows was not included, so the first executions took place on an open gallows erected in public view at the end of D.Wing.

The first condemned cell was located in D.Wing and a tunnel was constructed running from the base of D.Wing across to the Mater hospital to allow a Doctor to walk over to examine the executed prisoner.

The spectacle of public executions ceased in 1860, and in 1901 a new execution chamber was constructed at the bottom of C.Wing and this was used until the last hanging in the Gaol in 1961.

The tragic story of the seventeen hangings in the Gaol between 1901 and 1961, have been well documented and are available in various forms within the public domain.

For some warders the experience of having to do duties sitting with a condemned man could be emotional, no matter how hardened they were to death.

One lady recalled to historian Sean O 'Coinn in 2007:

"My Father who was a warder in the Crumlin Road Gaol, sat with a prisoner who was condemned to hang. Daddy came home at this time very upset and obviously affected by this whole experience. He fought in WW11 and seen much death and horror and was not a man to be easily shocked."

Another lady recalled a similar memory as a child:

"My Father had fought in WW1, serving in the Inniskilling Fusiliers. He was a warder in the Gaol and we lived in Court Street in 1939. I remember him saying to my Mother that

[seeing a man being hanged], was the most inhumane sight he had ever seen. I wouldn't wish it on anyone, he said."

The last two men to have the death sentence imposed on them were Liam Holden, aged nineteen, and Albert Browne, both in 1973 at the height of the recent conflict.

Liam Holden 1973.

However, on the 15th May, 1973, the capital punishment law was brought into line with Britain and the death penalty was removed from the statue books.

Had those two executions taken place, with the Gaol full of political prisoners, the British government knew it would have faced an even worst escalation of the conflict and further increasing critical judgement from the international community.

There were already 19,000 troops in the north and normal law no longer existed.

The northern administration had retained it on the statue books, long after it had been abolished in Britain. However, when the Northern Ireland government was suspended by Westminster in March 1972, direct rule was introduced from Westminster in London and thus the passing of law was now the sole responsibility of the British government until some form of self-government could be returned to the Stormont parliament in Belfast, that was representative of all the community, rather than a one-party dominated regime that was bias in favour of Unionist control.

External security at the Gaol and also at the Maze/Long Kesh prison primarily was the responsibility of the British Army.

There was also an army camp situated at the rear of the Gaol in Clifton Park Avenue, Girdwood Army Base. The 14-acre site was the home of 112 Field Squadron, 74 Engineer Regiment, a Territorial Regiment and also to the numerous regular battalions who were doing *tours* of North Belfast throughout the conflict, 1969-2007.

Members of the 10th Battalion, UDR also operated from Girdwood.

This base was also one of the main locations that men arrested on the day Internment was introduced on 9th August, 1971, were brought to for processing and interrogation, before transferring them into the adjoining Gaol.

The most critical years were during the early seventies between 1971 - 1974.

The IRA staged two major escapes in November and December 1971 despite the security that surrounded the Gaol. [Refer to Chapter 5]

One soldier, a Royal Marine, recalled:

> *"On my second tour in 1972, we were deployed to Girdwood in the New Lodge. During this time, we were briefed that prisoners in the Crumlin Road Gaol had rioted and taken prison officers prisoner, and that we were to go in and get them out, which we did after a bit of a battle".*

[40 Marine Commando was deployed to Girdwood in June to October 1972]

The same year on the 12th February 85 republican remand prisoners on C.Wing made an ambitious bid to escape from the Gaol.

They took a total of eight prison officers prisoner but their bid to escape en mass was thwarted by soldiers who had orders to shoot anyone who crossed the wall.

Each prison wing had their own exercise yard, which during the conflict had inner security and beyond that, there were outer perimeter security walls.

The British Army occupied *Sangers* – [watch-towers] at the front and rear of the Gaol and another Sanger was located close to the Gaol at the corner of Clifton Park Avenue and the Crumlin Road, which was an Outer-*Sanger* for Girdwood.

These Sangers were often modified in line as to the nature of attacks carried out by the IRA; whether it be gunfire, bombs, or rocket launchers.

The main entrance Sanger at Girdwood was modified to an SCS Sanger. It was

Prison Officers memorial removed from the Gaol after its closure in 1996. [Author] February 2009.

clad with a corrugated metal sheet, and had a steel rocket screen fitted; this increased the protection level against RPG'S only. They were normally built with high density concrete blocks.

The Girdwood compound was surrounded in reinforced concrete blast panels to mitigate against car bombs.

In the final years of the conflict Sanger duty was taken over by the UDR.

Girdwood Camp entrance after closure.

CHAPTER 7:
CLOSURE AND REGENERATION.

On the 31st August, 1994, the IRA announced a ceasefire and *"A cessation of all military operations"*. People in Nationalist districts took to the streets in celebration, while the newspapers hailed the headline, *"IT'S OVER"*.

The IRA in a five-paragraph communiqué stated that its decision to announce the ceasefire was *"In order to enhance the democratic process"*.

Six weeks later, Loyalists groups reciprocated the IRA communiqué, and in a statement read by Gusty Spence, it also announced a ceasefire.

It seemed hard to actually digest, *was it really over?*

When the reality of this historic announcement began to take effect, it was obvious that while the actual physical side of the conflict was at an end, the question was, how long it will take before stability would also become a reality. It would be a much greater task to win the peace, than win the war; although in this *war*, there were no winners, or losers, just the need to allow the "political endgame" to take its course.

Deep divisions and mistrust that spanned a generation *and well beyond*, would not suddenly disappear, but at least hopefully the killing was at an end, and all sides in the conflict would grasp the opportunity of a political settlement that would recognise the culture, the aspirations, and more important, the national identity of all involved.

There would have to be the will to embrace change, to acknowledge hurt, and also be prepared, to accept change. All sides needed to be pragmatic in any negotiations, and if all sides were to take ownership of any peace process, there needed to be inclusive talks, with no prior conditions.

Unfortunately, it became apparent, that peace was going to be *"a long rocky road"*, when political self-interest at Westminster by the then Conservative government, and unrealistic demands by the Unionists, began to take preference over peace, and cracks began to appear in the quest for a long-term agreement that would cement that peace.

Serious rioting broke out over Orange parades in Portadown that spread to other areas of The North, and it highlighted how fragile the cessation was.

The breaking point came when the government in London reliant on Unionist support in the House of Commons, [as it did not hold a sufficient majority], excluded Sinn Fein from the peace talks until the IRA disarmed.

Finally, on the 9th February, 1996, at 1800 hours-[6pm], an IRA communiqué, announced the end of its ceasefire. Within an hour, a huge bomb which had obviously been pre-planned exploded in London's Docklands, causing £140 million worth of damage.

Tension and shootings returned to the streets, but in a low key manner, in comparison to the years before the ceasefire. Perhaps this was a deliberate containment policy in the north, while another huge bomb attack was made against Britain on Saturday the 15th June, 1996; the target being Manchester city centre. The damage was estimated to be around £700 million, and 212 people were injured.

Against this concerning series of events, Crumlin Road Gaol had come to the end of its life as a *"working prison"*, closing the heavy gates of the *"air lock "* on the 31st, March 1996.

The Gaol fell silent, the cranking noise of closing gates, the vibrant movement along the landings, the clanging cell doors, the voices that laughed, or cursed, the smell that seemed to embed itself along the wings and settled in your nostrils, as you braced yourself for a routine that was regulated by the environment you were thrust into.

Smokers rolled their cigarettes, as the odour of *"slop out" oozed* itself along the Landing, amid the morning conversation, as men strolled toward the wash room, contemplating the idea of a *"greasy* "breakfast, and *the debatable mug of* tea.

Political prisoners had no work schedule, but a routine of sorts still needed to be followed, whether, self-driven, or as part of a command structure.

Warders changed shifts, Duty officers passed over their nightly reports, as the *"Crum"* began another day, were predictability was always open to question, and never *a given*.

Now suddenly; quietness, un-natural silence, only the ghosts were left to wander the Landings, as if to remind us that the past would not be allowed to be forgotten, no matter what the future held for this bleak, but impressive Victorian building.

Until then, only the ever-frequent mice would occupy the darkened, silent wings.

The political stalemate and renewed IRA bombings left the Gaol in limbo, as talks continued to try and regain the initiative that would reinstate the IRA ceasefire. They had let it be known that although it was committed to a political settlement, it still retained the ability to strike if required. Sinn Fein whose political electorate strength had continued to grow, needed to deliver a settlement that would be credible and acceptable to its military wing and maintain a united Republican Movement.

No side, the British, the Unionists, Nationalists or Republicans, were in a position of weakness, so it was necessary to take positive steps, that although may prove an electoral risk, could, at the same time, move the north back toward peace.

On Saturday 19th July 1997, at 12 noon, the IRA announced that from midday on Sunday 20th July - [Following Day], there would be a complete cessation of military operations. It was re-instating its ceasefire.

The following year, in what became known as the *"Good Friday Agreement"*, an agreement involving all sides of the conflict was signed to create a base of lasting peace.

It was hailed as a model peace accord, in reality, although it did guarantee peace, it was a *miss-mash* of contradiction, and was *"everything, to everybody"*. It failed to challenge the hard, difficult decisions, and that was to create further problems in the coming years.

Tolerance is not stability, but the accord was a major move in the right direction.

The quest for peace is not a single event, it is long process during which political threads become loose and unravelled and have to be patiently woven together again.

"The Long War", became *"The Long Peace"*, **that would take another ten years**, until 2007 before the words that *"The war is over"* became an official public declaration from the IRA, and the British declared *"Operation Banner"*, the British military deployment to the north-[Northern Ireland], was at an end.

While the politicians were engaged *"to and fro"* in the quest for future peace, the *future* of Crumlin Road Gaol was also a matter of discussion.

In August, 2003, the Gaol was transferred to the Office of the First Minister and Deputy First Minister for re-development under the Government's Reinvestment and Reform Initiative.

The future plans for the Gaol created some uncertainty on how best to utilise the ten-acre site, and it was a building that could cause controversy should the wrong approach be undertaken.

Finally in 2006, a unit from the Department of Social Development set up home in port cabin style offices on what was once A.Wings exercise yard.

Working in conjunction with *"Welcome Belfast"*, the Gaol opened its gates for tours at weekends through a *free* ticket booking scheme provided by the *Welcome Belfast* office.

These tours were primarily aimed at the community, rather than as a tourist initiative and it would gauge public interest in the prison, that could have a bearing on the future direction tha plans for the Gaol would take.

A small number of guides were brought in to conduct the tours and given a prepared script to learn, that excluded any political reference to the *recent conflict*. Considering that the Gaol was steeped in political history. * *"it was a rigid safeguard that was perhaps too cautious, but at the beginning of the initiative, understandable"*. *[John Quinn, one of the guides involved at that time 2006]

The amount of people who queued outside the Gaol each Saturday and Sunday morning, took everyone by surprise; the interest and the numbers wanting to *"get in"* to the *"Crum"*, ran into thousands over the passing months.

The Gaol was more-or-less as it was left in 1996. The tours were restricted to an hour, due to the high numbers booking, and seven guides, - [three, sometimes four], would do five tours each, per day.

The tour consisted of: The Air Lock, the Reception area, Admin Block - [Governor's Corridor], the Circle, the Tunnel, then C.Wing, the Condemned Cell, and then over to the Burial Site-[Old Garden area], and FINISH. Tours were back-to back and had to be completed within the hour. Each group on the tours, were a complete mix of backgrounds; you were simply put on whatever tour had free spaces.

One of the guides who was there at the beginning and conducted regular tours for three years under the DSD was historian, John Quinn.

He recollected those early tours beginning in 2006:

"When we first began, you could feel there was a sense of caution in how the narrative would be presented, they were sensitive to the history of the Gaol"

Which I totally understood being a historian and particularly knowing the history of the Gaol myself, they were keen to avoid any controversy.

I read the script and it covered the early penal system, the Suffragettes, daily routine and the executions. I knew from the beginning that the people coming through those gates, were in the main, "Locals", many of whom, were either former political prisoners, or staff, and those who were not, would want to hear and learn from a narrative that included the conflict.

I decided to impose my own personality on to the tours, keeping in the main-[at the beginning] to the run of the script, but *"drip-feeding"* early political history into the narrative. It worked, because the feedback I was getting at the end of the tours, justified my stance.

I lobbied for political history to be included and the general feedback and demand from those coming on the tours, strengthened the argument. After a while, they relented and said, just be careful of how you present it. For me personally, *I did not work to a script*, I knew the history of the Gaol and thankfully the feedback I was getting in the Visitor's Book that they eventfully introduced, was very complementary of my tours.

A few of the guides were happy to stick with the original script, so each tour was different depending on the guide you got. I know that people were *hooking themselves* on to my tours; some people who knew me, would also try and get allocated on to one of my tours, if they saw me. It was nice to be regarded in that manner.

It was all to do with the narrative, the humour and the history.

As time progressed, they began to facilitate "Special mid-week" tours for political related groups, or Community groups. I, and another guide, Ken, were brought in to do these special political tours.

Up until the end of 2009, which was our last year before the DSD relinquished their role in the tours to allow for the restoration program to begin, I must have brought several thousand people around the Gaol over a three-year period.

I personally brought several Republican and Loyalist groups around the Gaol; an Ex- Prison officers' group, several politicians, and the media, that included, UTV - [Ulster Television] presented by Paul Clark, an Australian film crew making a documentary about prison escapes, BBC Radio Ulster *"Your Place and Mine"*, the *Irish News* newspaper and others I can't recall".

> *"The only annoying part during the normal weekend tours was that you were bringing around such a diverse mixture of people and at the end of the tour, you never got the chance to talk to anyone, as you had to go straight to the gate and begin your next tour."*

I recall one morning being brought in for a special tour and awaiting the group, the back gates opened and three black taxis and two cars rolled in; it was Gerry Adams and his family, along with friends. For me, it was just another tour! I remember him playing with the grandchildren on C.Wing.

On another occasion, I, along with Ken again, where brought in for another Special tour. We mingled around the front of the *"Air-Lock"* talking to a group from North Antrim, part of a DUP – [Democratic Unionist Party], constituency outing, when the doors of the Admin block opened, and there with outstretched arms, Ian Paisley appeared, and in that distinctive preacher voice, proclaimed with a wide smile, *"Welcome to Crumlin Road Gaol".*

I was waiting on them all, dropping on one knee!!

At the end of the tour, they gathered for a group photograph on the wing, as most groups would do. I discreetly stood to the side waiting to bring them back to the front, when again, I heard that distinctive voice:

"That man there, come into the photograph".

Somewhere up in North Antrim, there is a DUP visit to the *"Crum"*, with me *stuck in it!*

I'm sure Ken was also in it. I don't remember what year that was.

I would never change, or revise my narrative, no matter who was on a tour. It was historically correct, balanced, and did not gloss over the facts.

However, the one thing that I could not give them, no matter how good the tours may have been, was the noise, the smell and the atmosphere that existed on that wing. The quietness, simply did not reflect the reality.

I think that the Gaol is now maybe *"too sanitised"*, but, at the same time, I appreciate the issues of Health & Safety.

On one occasion, a former Loyalist prisoner, asked me *"John, what about our escapes?"*

"I had a tunnel in my cell, it didn't go too far, it was caught!"

It was in good humour and I just smiled.

[It didn't make it into my narrative on escapes, but they deserve credit for attempting a tunnel.]

In August, 2010, the Gaol closed for major renovation work and was contracted out to be run as a tourist visitor attraction. It was upgraded to facilitate tourist groups, provide entertainment and conference facilities for the local community, and a restaurant, called *"Cuffs"*, along with a gift shop, were opened.

The heavy metal *"Air-Lock"* entrance has been removed and the entrance has returned to its original façade; the watch towers, Sangers, and much of the exterior security walls are gone. It no longer, [on the outside] resembles the Gaol of the recent conflict.

The prison chapel is now a conference centre and various cultural and art exhibitions are often a feature of the Gaol.

The Gaol has become a popular visitor attraction and people from all over the world are now coming to visit and experience the once notorious *Crumlin Road Gaol.*

Aerial Photo Belfast Prison

Leading to the Basement of D. Wing. Photo: 25-4-09. [Author].

D.Wing, Self-explanatory !!! [Author]